Differentiating for Inclusion

Target Ladders:

Autistic Spectrum

Louise Nelson

Series editor Kate Ruttle

LDA has a range of learning development aids to help children with special needs and general learning difficulties. For our full range and helpful information, visit www.ldalearning.com.

Target Ladders: Autistic Spectrum

ISBN 978-1-85503-549-2

© Louise Nelson 2013

All Rights Reserved

First published 2013
Reprinted 2014
Printed in the UK for LDA by Page Bros, Norwich

LDA, Findel Education, Hyde Buildings, Ashton Road, Hyde, Cheshire, SK14 4SH

Contents

Closing the gap

Although schools are trying to reduce the number of children on their Special Educational Need (SEN) registers, the array of learning difficulties faced by the children is not changing or diminishing. In many areas, the responsibility for identifying learning difficulties, and supporting the children, is being thrust more onto schools because the external services hitherto available to support identification and remediation are fast disappearing. In most primary schools, the responsibility for tackling children's learning challenges continues to lie with class teachers and Special Educational Needs Co-ordinators (SENCos), many of whom are non-specialists.

Since 2012, reporting on children's behaviour and the way in which it is managed in schools has been a separate category in the Ofsted Evaluation Schedule. Behaviour, whether or not it is linked to an SEN, is now recognised as playing a significant part in children's learning. Inspectors are now looking for evidence that schools are working to 'close the gap' and that there is improvement in behaviour for learning over time, including for children on the Autistic Spectrum (AS).

Case study

An AS child in Year 4 had the target to *'stop hurting other children in the playground'*. The child did not understand that others were being hurt, as he felt his rough play was merely play. The target was therefore unachievable over the time period (one term) in which it had been expected to be met. Therefore, adults modelled and directed the child to appropriate behaviours in the playground and engaged the child in play with chosen role models. They also directed the peers to indicate firmly and directly that the child's play was becoming too rough and that he needed to stop. A target was set involving sharing play equipment by turn-taking with one peer, while being monitored by an adult. Once the child could achieve this smaller step he could then move on to join a larger group and was gradually integrated into the playground over a period of time (with appropriate verbal reminders before each play) using his new and appropriate play skills. Both he and his peers had a more enjoyable playtime.

Whether individual targets are recorded on an Individual Education Plan (IEP), an internal target sheet, a Record of Progress (RoP) or by some other mechanism, the fact remains that these children continue to need small-steps targets in order to clarify learning priorities and give the children a sense of achievement when they tick off another target.

The *Target Ladders* titles focus on one SEN at a time, in order that the range of difficulties and challenges facing young people with that SEN can be acknowledged. If any child in your care has any of the behaviours or difficulties addressed by a book in the series, then the targets listed in that book should be helpful and appropriate.

The *Target Ladders* books aim to support you in the following ways:

- Focusing on what a child can do, rather than what they cannot do, in order to identify next steps.
- Presenting 'small steps' targets for children.
- Suggesting strategies and activities you may find helpful in order to achieve the targets.
- Giving you the information you need to use your professional judgement and understanding of the child in determining priorities for learning.
- Recognising that every child is different and will follow their own pathway through the targets.
- Giving you an overview of the range of difficulties experienced by children with a particular SEN. Not all children will experience all of the difficulties, but once you know and understand the implications of the SEN, it gives you a better understanding as to a child's learning priorities.
- Providing a system for setting and monitoring targets which can replace or complement IEPs.

Setting useful targets for a child can be tricky. But '*He doesn't play with other children*' is not a constructive statement when deciding what the next steps should be. In order to support the child, you need to find out first what they *can* do already and then break down the next steps. You are then in a good position to set targets and consider interventions.

Case study

A Year 2 child shouted at peers and adults. His target was to '*stop shouting in school*'. The child found this confusing, as he sometimes saw other children and adults shouting in school, for example, on sports day or when a pantomime was being performed. He didn't understand why this rule had been broken. The target was changed to '*use a talking voice in the classroom*'. Adults worked with the child to practise using a shouting and a talking voice, and talked about when each should be used. A visual resource representing a volume control was used to indicate the different voices: whisper, talking and shouting. Before a special event the child was prepared for the voice which would be appropriate. In some instances, when the child (in excitement) was unaware that his voice had increased in volume, adults used the language '*You are shouting, stop, use a talking voice*'. As a result the child learned to use appropriate voices and was not constantly told to be quiet.

Using the *Target Ladders* books will enable both non-specialist teachers and SENCos to identify appropriate learning goals for independent learning, to adapt the suggested strategies or ideas for their own pupils, and to begin to impact on the way in which children on the Autistic Spectrum access the school curriculum in order to close the gap between these children and their peers.

How to use this book

You will find a simple five-step summary of how to use this book on page 9.

Every child diagnosed as being on the Autistic Spectrum (AS), including Asperger Syndrome and Socio-Communication Disorders, has different strengths and weaknesses. The priority for addressing these will be determined by the difficulties currently being faced by the child and will depend on your professional judgement, supported by the child's current anxieties.

In order to support you with focused target setting, the book is structured as follows:

- Seven different Aspects of the Autistic Spectrum have been identified (see Fig. 1 opposite). Think about the child's difficulties: which of these Aspects is causing most concern at the moment?
- Within each Aspect there are three or four different Target Ladders, each based on a particular area of challenge. This is intended to help you to think carefully about precisely where the barrier may be.
- The relevant Target Ladder can then be used to identify the 'next step' target for the child.
- Suggested activities and strategies offer classroom-friendly ideas so you can support the child to meet their target.

For example, as you can see in the chart opposite, difficulties with Aspect 4: 'Managing change' can be subdivided into four specific areas to work on: Change within the classroom, Change across the day, Moving to a new class/school and Dealing with the unexpected. Each of these four Target Ladders contains up to 28 targets.

Aspects, Target Ladders and Targets

Aspects

The seven different Aspects of the Autistic Spectrum identified in this book describe contexts and difficulties which are frequently faced by children diagnosed as being on the Autistic Spectrum. In order to identify the most appropriate Aspect for a particular child, you will need to consider the aspect of a child's behaviour which is either particularly challenging or which is a barrier to their learning or integration. The priority when deciding which of the Aspects is most important will come from an understanding of the child's current behaviours and where the most urgent challenges are presented.

The Aspects of the Autistic Spectrum identified in this book are:

1 Social interaction: friendships
2 Social interaction: relationships
3 Getting attention
4 Managing change
5 Personal organisation
6 Managing feelings
7 Non-verbal interaction.

Target Ladders

Each of the Aspects is further subdivided into three or four Target Ladders, each of which addresses different parts of the Aspect. These enable you to develop your understanding of the child's individual needs, 'drilling down' to assist you to identify the child's particular strengths and weaknesses. The Target Ladders are set out on pages 40–95.

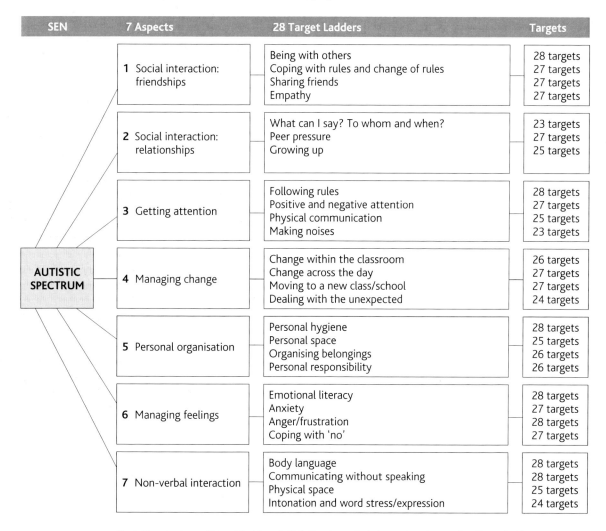

SEN	7 Aspects	28 Target Ladders	Targets
AUTISTIC SPECTRUM	1 Social interaction: friendships	Being with others Coping with rules and change of rules Sharing friends Empathy	28 targets 27 targets 27 targets 27 targets
	2 Social interaction: relationships	What can I say? To whom and when? Peer pressure Growing up	23 targets 27 targets 25 targets
	3 Getting attention	Following rules Positive and negative attention Physical communication Making noises	28 targets 27 targets 25 targets 23 targets
	4 Managing change	Change within the classroom Change across the day Moving to a new class/school Dealing with the unexpected	26 targets 27 targets 27 targets 24 targets
	5 Personal organisation	Personal hygiene Personal space Organising belongings Personal responsibility	28 targets 25 targets 26 targets 26 targets
	6 Managing feelings	Emotional literacy Anxiety Anger/frustration Coping with 'no'	28 targets 27 targets 28 targets 27 targets
	7 Non-verbal interaction	Body language Communicating without speaking Physical space Intonation and word stress/expression	28 targets 28 targets 25 targets 24 targets

Fig. 1: The structure of *Target Ladders: Autistic Spectrum*. Each Aspect has three or four Target Ladders, each with up to 28 targets.

Targets

There are up to 28 targets in each Target Ladder, with the simplest labelled with the letter 'A', then moving through the alphabet up to 'N', which are the most difficult. Pairs of targets, identified by the same letter, present a similar level of challenge. So, for example, all of the targets marked E are at approximately the same level of development, which is slightly easier than F and slightly harder than D. Since each child is individual, some children will achieve harder targets before they do easier ones – and no child would be expected to work their way through all of the targets.

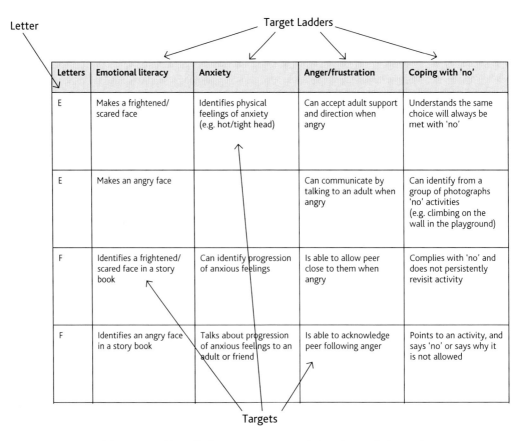

Fig. 2: Part of the Target Ladders table for Aspect 6: Managing feelings (page 82), showing how targets are structured in the ladders.

However, it is not necessarily the case that the targets in row E for each Aspect are at the same developmental level, because the Aspects are so different. Thus, a child may have a target from row E in Aspect 4: Managing change but a target from row H in Aspect 6: Managing feelings.

The targets are all written in positive language. This is to support you when you:

- look through them to find out what the child *can already* do;
- use them as the basis of the target you set for the child.

As you track the statements through each ladder, identifying what the child can already do, be aware of missed steps. If a child has missed one of the steps, further progress up that ladder may be insecure. Many children learn to mask the missed step, using developing skills in other areas to help them, but the time may come when the missed step will cause difficulties.

Activities and strategies to achieve the targets

In the Target Ladders on pages 40–95, targets are listed on left-hand pages. The corresponding right-hand pages offer ideas for activities or strategies that you might use to help to achieve the targets. These are suggestions only – but they have all been used successfully in classrooms and are accepted good practice. Here, however, the activities or strategies are shown at the point in the developmental process at which they are likely to make the most impact.

The suggested activities can often be adapted to work for a range of targets within this stage of the ladder. For this reason, activities are generally not linked to individual targets.

How to set targets: A five-step summary

1. **Use Fig. 1 on page 7 to identify the one or two Aspects of the Autistic Spectrum that are most challenging for the child.**

2. **Turn to the Scope and Sequence Charts on pages 11–18.** These charts will help you pinpoint the specific targets you need – a more detailed explanation is given on page 11. The Scope and Sequence charts show the *upper limit* of the targets reached in each Target Ladder in each Aspect. Use these to gain an indication of where in the book you are likely to find appropriate targets.

3. **In the Target Ladders tables on pages 40–95, locate the targets** that you have identified from the Scope and Sequence charts and pinpoint specific ones for the child to work towards.

4. **Photocopy or print out from the CD the relevant targets page** so that you can:
   ○ highlight and date those the child can already do;
   ○ identify the next priorities.

5. **Use the Record of Progress sheet on page 20** to create a copy of the targets for the child or their parents.

Making the most of Target Ladders

You may find the following tips helpful when setting your targets.

- If you are not sure which Aspect to highlight for a child:
  ○ think about your main concerns about that child's learning;
  ○ talk to the child about what they would like to improve;
  ○ discuss targets with the child's parents/carers.

A target that the child wants to improve is more likely to be successful.

- Once you have identified the Aspect, use the Scope and Sequence charts on pages 12–18 to identify the most beneficial Target Ladder and to ascertain which page to start on.
  - Look for any 'missed steps', and target those first. The child is likely to find success fairly quickly and will be motivated to continue to try to reach new targets.
  - Talk to the child and agree an appropriate target based on your skills inventory. Again, targets which the child is aware of tend to be achieved most quickly and are motivational.
- The target does not have to be the lowest unachieved statement in any ladder: use your professional judgement and knowledge of the child to identify the most useful and important target for the child.
- No child will follow all of the targets in precisely the order listed. Use your professional judgement, and your knowledge about what the child can already do, to identify the most appropriate target and be realistic in your expectations. There may be some zigzagging up and down a column.
- When setting targets, always ask yourself practical questions:
  - What can I change in order to enable the child to meet the targets?
  - Which people and resources are available to support the child?
  - What is the likelihood of a child achieving a target within the next month or so?
  - Which targets have been agreed with other children in the class?

It is important that the targets you set are realistic considering the time, the adult support and the resources available.

Once you have identified what the child can already achieve, continue to highlight and update the sheets each time the child achieves a new target. Celebrate progress with the child – while, at the same time, constantly checking to ensure that previously achieved targets remain secure. If any target becomes insecure, revisit it briefly, without setting a formal target, in order to give the child an opportunity to consolidate the skill without feeling that they are going backwards in their achievements.

Scope and Sequence charts

The Scope and Sequence charts can be used to help you to pinpoint targets, following the advice on the preceding pages. Once you have identified the Aspect(s) you wish to focus on:

1. Find the relevant page in the Scope and Sequence charts on pages 12–18. Look for the Aspect name here:

2. Identify the Target Ladder(s) that matches the skills you wish to target. Look for the names of the ladders here:

3. Read down the list of targets here: The targets shown here are the highest for the ladder on that page. If the first target listed is too easy, look at the next target beneath it. Continue down the list until you reach a target that is beyond the child's current attainment.

4. Find the page number, shown here: Turn to that page and read all the targets on it. One of them should be appropriate. If not, turn to the previous or subsequent page.

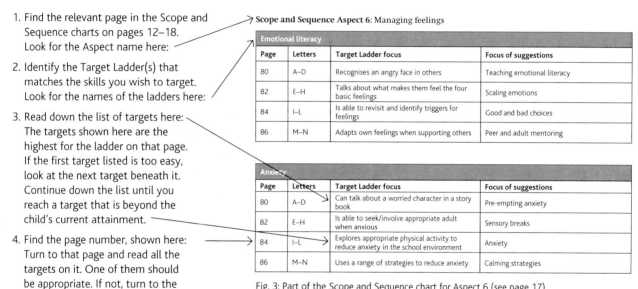

Scope and Sequence Aspect 6: Managing feelings

Emotional literacy

Page	Letters	Target Ladder focus	Focus of suggestions
80	A–D	Recognises an angry face in others	Teaching emotional literacy
82	E–H	Talks about what makes them feel the four basic feelings	Scaling emotions
84	I–L	Is able to revisit and identify triggers for feelings	Good and bad choices
86	M–N	Adapts own feelings when supporting others	Peer and adult mentoring

Anxiety

Page	Letters	Target Ladder focus	Focus of suggestions
80	A–D	Can talk about a worried character in a story book	Pre-empting anxiety
82	E–H	Is able to seek/involve appropriate adult when anxious	Sensory breaks
84	I–L	Explores appropriate physical activity to reduce anxiety in the school environment	Anxiety
86	M–N	Uses a range of strategies to reduce anxiety	Calming strategies

Fig. 3: Part of the Scope and Sequence chart for Aspect 6 (see page 17).

Bear in mind the following:

- The wording of the target may not be precisely accurate for your child. Modify it to make it appropriate.
- Different children may meet the target statements in a slightly different order. The order shown is approximate and true for many children. Adapt the order in which you set the targets for the individual child.
- No child is expected to have all of the targets on the page. A range of small-steps targets is shown in order to give you the widest possible variety of targets from which to select.
- If you cannot find a target which meets your needs, use the other targets to give you an idea of the level expected, and write your own target. It is important that all of the targets on the Record of Progress are appropriate for the individual child.

Scope and Sequence Aspect 1: Social interaction: friendships

Being with others

Page	Letters	Target Ladder focus	Focus of suggestions
40	A–D	Plays alone in shared space	Sharing with others
42	E–H	Leads, follows or starts play	Sharing with one child
44	I–L	Can sometimes consider other group members	Understanding points of view
46	M–N	Accepts that sometimes you may win and at other times may lose	Social skills groups

Coping with rules and change of rules

Page	Letters	Target Ladder focus	Focus of suggestions
40	A–D	Makes requests of peers – repetitive play	Modelling appropriate language
42	E–H	Willingly joins in familiar games with familiar rules	Sharing with more than one child
44	I–L	Is able to respond to rule changes with appropriate language	Following rules
46	M–N	Is willing to play again after defeat	Comic strip conversations

Sharing friends

Page	Letters	Target Ladder focus	Focus of suggestions
40	A–D	Plays alongside friend, engaged in play with other involving talk	Taking turns
42	E–H	Offers assistance when friend needs help (not all the time)	Communicating with others
44	I–L	Understands that friendship is reciprocal	Expressing feelings appropriately
46	M–N	Shows respect for views of friends	Circle of Friends

Empathy

Page	Letters	Target Ladder focus	Focus of suggestions
40	A–D	Involved in exchange of ideas and information	Modelling appropriate language
42	E–H	Offers appropriate verbal response to comfort others	Communicating with others
44	I–L	Can sometimes accept things not happening as expected	Following rules
46	M–N	Respects others and uses appropriate language	Circle of Friends

Scope and Sequence Aspect 2: Social interaction: relationships

What can I say? To whom and when?

Page	Letters	Target Ladder focus	Focus of suggestions
48	A–D	Makes simple social requests to peers	Asking for things
50	E–H	Makes statements of preferred option with wider peer group and familiar adults	Making requests and offering suggestions
52	I–L	Can approach unfamiliar others for information	Social kissing and hugging
54	M–N	Knows it is inappropriate to ask unfamiliar people about private or personal information	Talking to unfamiliar others

Peer pressure

Page	Letters	Target Ladder focus	Focus of suggestions
48	A–D	Can make own choice, differing from peers	Making independent choices
50	E–H	Identifies wrong choices	Right and wrong choices
52	I–L	Adheres to boundaries for inappropriate language	Social language
54	M–N	Can talk about risk and how to make a good choice	Identifying risk

Growing up

Page	Letters	Target Ladder focus	Focus of suggestions
48	A–D	Matches own sex to picture of unclothed boy or girl	Introducing gender
50	E–H	Understands greetings of unfamiliar others	Welcoming classroom visitors
52	I–L	Understands simple emotional/hormonal changes in bodies of opposite sex and approximately when they occur	Modesty
54	M–N	Understands areas of others' bodies that are inappropriate to touch	Puberty

Scope and Sequence Aspect 3: Getting attention

	Following rules		
Page	**Letters**	**Target Ladder focus**	**Focus of suggestions**
56	A–D	Keeps hands and feet to self independently	Using a system of rewards
58	E–H	Sits appropriately in assembly for 10 minutes	Following rules
60	I–L	Understands why rules exist for games (sport)	Following rules
62	M	Generalises rules	Rules in sport Safety

	Positive and negative attention		
Page	**Letters**	**Target Ladder focus**	**Focus of suggestions**
56	A–D	Responds to verbal/visual prompting and pauses negative behaviours	Reinforcing rules
58	E–H	Understands negative body language in others	Positive and negative attention
60	I–L	Controls voice volume when seeking attention	Voice – volume control
62	M–N	Takes responsibility for own (negative or positive) behaviour	Using rating scales/feelings thermometers

	Physical communication		
Page	**Letters**	**Target Ladder focus**	**Focus of suggestions**
56	A–D	Taps arm of peer to gain attention	Oral and physical communication
58	E–H	Moves face of adult towards self	Inappropriate physical contact
60	I–L	Knows not to push peers	Discussing inappropriate behaviours
62	M–N	Knows not to lean on adult heavily	Using rating scales/feelings thermometers

	Making noises		
Page	**Letters**	**Target Ladder focus**	**Focus of suggestions**
56	B–D	Laughs to show pleasure	Oral and physical communication
58	E–H	Knows which behaviours are irritating	Sustained inappropriate behaviours
60	I–K	Knows not to distract others	Discussing inappropriate behaviours
62	M–N	Accepts consequences for swearing at adults	Swearing

Scope and Sequence Aspect 4: Managing change

Change within the classroom

Page	Letters	Target Ladder focus	Focus of suggestions
64	A–D	Recognises own belongings even if they are not where expected	Managing routines
66	E–H	Works/plays with other peers independently if friend is absent	Prepare for disappointment
68	I–L	Uses personal strategies for preparing for and managing changes	Preparing for change
70	M–N	Understands and copes with unexpected change	Planning for change

Change across the day

Page	Letters	Target Ladder focus	Focus of suggestions
64	A–D	Returns to classroom after playtime independently	Managing change between activities
66	E–H	Changes clothes for PE independently using visual prompts if necessary	Change across the day
68	I–L	Uses strategies to manage anxiety and talks about them with peers	Managing anxiety
70	M–N	Suggests strategies for others to help understand and cope with unexpected change	Planning for change

Moving to a new class/school

Page	Letters	Target Ladder focus	Focus of suggestions
64	A–D	Associates familiar peers with school	Unexpected visitors or changes
66	E–H	Identifies new classroom from photo and talks about it	Moving to a new school or classroom
68	I–L	Discusses possible concerns/anxieties with peers and adults	Moving school
70	M–N	Attends new intake days and uses strategies for independent coping skills	Managing anxiety

Dealing with the unexpected

Page	Letters	Target Ladder focus	Focus of suggestions
64	A–D	Complies and participates fully	Unexpected visitors or changes
66	E–H	Understands that everything is not always certain	Prepare for disappointment
68	I–L	Talks through a range of strategies and selects appropriate one to apply and shares suggestions	Managing anxiety
70	M–N	Has a range of strategies for personal coping skills	Managing anxiety

Scope and Sequence Aspect 5: Personal organisation

Personal hygiene

Page	Letters	Target Ladder focus	Focus of suggestions
72	A–D	Uses toilet independently	Toilet training
74	E–H	Is able to change discreetly for PE	Uses visuals for personal hygiene
76	I–L	Can make decisions to wash appropriately and independently	Understanding hygiene Growing up
78	M–N	Knows how and where to use appropriate products associated with puberty	Approaching puberty

Personal space

Page	Letters	Target Ladder focus	Focus of suggestions
72	A–D	Takes turns if prompted and guided by an adult	Sharing with peers
74	E–H	Shares resources in a small group and allows others to use desired item; waits turn	Making choices
76	I–L	Understands the more familiar the other, the smaller the personal space becomes	Personal space
78	M–N	Can ask for own personal space if necessary	Personal space social skills groups

Organising belongings

Page	Letters	Target Ladder focus	Focus of suggestions
72	A–D	Returns water bottle to correct place once used	Developing routines
74	E–H	Can return own belongings/clothing to own PE/swimming bag independently	Visual prompts for organisation
76	I–L	Is aware that different belongings are needed on different days	Organisation
78	M–N	Relies on homework planner for prompting	Developing strategies for organising

Personal responsibility

Page	Letters	Target Ladder focus	Focus of suggestions
72	A–D	Follows simple routines and instructions with verbal and visual prompting	Developing routines
74	E–H	Knows that making excuses or blaming others is inappropriate	Taking responsibility
76	I–L	Is trustworthy and takes care of others' belongings	Responsibility
78	M–N	Shows parents that they can be trusted	Confidences

Scope and Sequence Aspect 6: Managing feelings

Emotional literacy

Page	Letters	Target Ladder focus	Focus of suggestions
80	A–D	Recognises an angry face in others	Teaching emotional literacy
82	E–H	Talks about what makes them feel the four basic feelings	Scaling emotions
84	I–L	Is able to revisit and identify triggers for feelings	Good and bad choices
86	M–N	Adapts own feelings when supporting others	Peer and adult mentoring

Anxiety

Page	Letters	Target Ladder focus	Focus of suggestions
80	A–D	Can talk about a worried character in a story book	Pre-empting anxiety
82	E–H	Is able to seek/involve appropriate adult when anxious	Sensory breaks
84	I–L	Explores appropriate physical activity to reduce anxiety in the school environment	Anxiety
86	M–N	Uses a range of strategies to reduce anxiety	Calming strategies

Anger/frustration

Page	Letters	Target Ladder focus	Focus of suggestions
80	A–D	Knows what makes friends angry	Coping with anger
82	E–H	Begins to recognise stages of own anger using a number scale	Scaling emotions
84	I–L	Uses strategies successfully to reduce anger	Strategies for controlling emotions
86	M–N	Accepts and understands 'no' from unfamiliar peer	Identifying triggers

Coping with 'no'

Page	Letters	Target Ladder focus	Focus of suggestions
80	A–D	Accepts the consequences of saying 'no'	Teaching 'no'
82	E–H	Revisits and talks about responses to 'no'	Anger management
84	I–L	Accepts 'no' without inappropriate facial response or gesture	Good and bad choices
86	M–N	Can talk about the reasons for adults saying 'no' and what this means and how to respond	Peer and adult mentoring

Scope and Sequence Aspect 7: Non-verbal interaction

Body language

Page	Letters	Target Ladder focus	Focus of suggestions
88	A–D	Recognises arms wide as encouragement for a hug	Understanding rewards
90	E–H	Can tell if an adult's body stance is negative and disapproving	Supporting non-verbal communication
92	I–L	Can use 'stop' signal	Body language
94	M–N	Reacts appropriately to aggressive body language	Responding to aggression

Communicating without speaking

Page	Letters	Target Ladder focus	Focus of suggestions
88	A–D	Tries to imitate syllables	Verbalisation
90	E–H	Initiates interaction using a range of up to ten basic signs, using PECS or Makaton	Makaton PECS
92	I–L	Communicates to a range of peers using PECS/Makaton	Augmentative and Alternative Communication
94	M–N	Communicates simply with familiar peers in selected social situations	Tricky social situations

Physical space

Page	Letters	Target Ladder focus	Focus of suggestions
88	A–D	Knows not to lean on people without reminders	Sitting and leaning
90	E–H	Allows peers to have personal space on carpet	Encouraging understanding of personal space
92	I–L	Knows how much personal space is needed in different contexts	Personal space
94	M–N	Responds appropriately to unexpected invasion of own personal space and that of others	Tricky social situations

Intonation and word stress/expression

Page	Letters	Target Ladder focus	Focus of suggestions
88	A–D	Copies intonation during echolalia (repeated speed or verbal sounds)	Imitating intonation
90	E–H	Uses rising intonation for questions	
92	I–L	Asks questions to check the meaning of idioms	Talking and 'speed dating'
94	M–N	Uses sarcasm by elongated words	Sarcasm and idioms

Records of Progress

Creating a Record of Progress

Arrange to meet with the child and ask them first to tell you what they are good at. Record their responses on the Record of Progress (RoP). A blank form is supplied for you to copy on page 20 and on the CD. Ask the child then to tell you which areas they would most like to improve. If it is appropriate, choose something that addresses at least one of their issues as a target, so that the child feels some ownership of their RoP. If your school operates a Pupil Passport system, then you may want to amend the RoP form, but you will need a sheet that can be annotated and amended.

As you add one or two more targets, talk to the child to check that they agree that each target is relevant and that they understand what they will need to do to achieve their targets. Targets that children do not know or care about are much harder for them to achieve. Limit the number of targets to a maximum of three. Remember, you do not need to use the precise wording of the targets given in this book: adapt the words to match the maturity and understanding of the learner.

If you are planning to use a published intervention, check to see what the recommended length of time for the intervention is. Monitor the impact of the intervention (see page 21) and review at regular intervals – at least half-termly – to see if there is an impact. If not, consider whether a different intervention would be more effective.

Principles for the effective use of a RoP include the following:

- The form must be 'live'. The child will need to have access to it at all times, as will all adults who work with the child, in order that it can be referred to, amended and updated regularly. It would be good practice to send a copy home for the parents/carers. If you think that the child is likely to lose or destroy their RoP, make a photocopy so that you can supply another.
- Together with the child, you have identified their priority areas to focus on. Management and support for these should be consistent across the school day and from all adults.
- As soon as each target has been achieved, according to the success criteria you agreed, the form should be dated and a 'next step' considered.
- When you set up the RoP, select a review date which is ideally about half a term ahead and no more than a term ahead. Don't wait until this date to identify that targets have been achieved, but on this date review progress towards all targets – or identified next steps – and agree new targets.
- If a target has not been achieved, consider why not. If possible, try a different approach to meeting the target. Having the same target over and over is likely to bore the child and put them off following their RoP.

RECORD OF PROGRESS

Name _____ Class _____ Date agreed _____ Review date _____

My targets are	I will know that I have achieved my target when I can	Date when I achieved my target	Next steps

I am good at			
I would like to be better at			
It helps me when			

RoP number: _____ Targets approved by: Pupil _____ Teacher _____

SENCo _____ Parent/Carer _____ TA _____

Using Target Ladders

Monitoring a Record of Progress

In order to ensure that your Record of Progress (RoP) is used effectively, you need to monitor progress towards the targets each time you offer support. Use a monitoring sheet; a photocopiable example is given on page 22 and on the CD.

- Use a separate sheet – copied on to a different colour of paper – for each target.
- Write the child's name at the top of the sheet and the target underneath.
- On each occasion when someone works with the child towards the target, they should write the smaller, more specific target that you are working towards *during this session* in the box.
- They should then write a comment. On each occasion the child achieves the target during the session and then back in class, tick the box.

Comments should, as far as possible, refer to the child's behaviour and attitude rather than to their learning, which should be celebrated during the session. The intention is that these sheets should be used to create a cumulative record of a child's progress towards their target. The evidence here can be used to assess the impact of an intervention in order that its appropriateness can be evaluated swiftly and any additional actions can be taken promptly.

What precisely you record will depend on the type of support being offered and the nature of the target.

- If you are delivering a planned intervention, make a record of the unit/page/activity and a comment about the learning the child demonstrated. For example, a comment relating to a target about the child's ability to share might read: '*Initially, shared glue stick with SH for 2 mins. Then refused to share.*'
- If you are offering support in the classroom, you might want to comment on the child's learning over a few lessons. Focus on what the child has achieved in the lessons and whether the learning is secure.
- As a general principle, aim to include more positive than negative comments, and always try to balance a negative with a positive comment.

At the half-termly review of the RoP, collect together all of the monitoring sheets and look at the frequency of the comments against each target as well as the learning they reflect. If a child has had absences, or an intervention has not happened as often as planned, consider what impact that has had on the effectiveness of the intervention. If the intervention has gone as planned, look at the progress charted and ask yourself these questions:

- Is it swift enough? Is the intervention helping this child to close the gap? Is the adult working with the child the best person for the job?
- Is this the best intervention? Is there anything else you can reasonably do in school?
- What should happen next? If the intervention was successful, do you continue it, develop it, consolidate it or change to a different target?

At the end of the process, create a new RoP with the child and make a new monitoring sheet.

Monitoring the progress of _____ towards meeting

Target _____

Date	Target	Comment	Achieved			

Using Target Ladders

What is the Autistic Spectrum?

The National Autistic Society (http://www.autism.org.uk) defines Autism as follows:

> **Autism is a complex neurodevelopmental disorder, marked by multiple symptoms that include atypicalities in:**
>
> - social interactions (i.e. people with autism would often find it difficult to understand others' mental states and emotions, and respond accordingly)
> - verbal and non-verbal communication
> - repetitive behaviour (i.e. people with autism might repeat certain words or actions over and over, usually in a rigid rule-governed manner).

Autism is complex and is in general diagnosed by a paediatrician. If a child receives a diagnosis, this is a lifelong condition, and means they may experience difficulties in three areas, the so-called triad of differences or impairment.

Fig. 4: The 'triad of differences' in Autism.

Communication
Children with AS have difficulties when communicating with others, including both verbal and non-verbal misunderstandings and difficulties. Unlike the typically developing child, they require direct teaching and modelling in order to acquire these communication skills. AS children may find it difficult to understand the use of social language, jokes and sarcastic comments, as they may interpret these literally. They may also have difficulty processing language used in the classroom and everyday situations.

Thought and behaviour
Children with AS have difficulty moving on from rigid behaviours and may develop all-consuming obsessions. For example, a child in school may be unable to move on from the computer game they have been playing and is constantly thinking about trying to achieve the next level. AS children may have difficulty coping with changes in routines and generalising skills learned in one environment. For example, the child who is able to accurately work though mathematical calculations using money in the classroom may be unable to transfer this skill to a real-life situation in a shop.

Social interaction
AS children experience great difficulties in social situations, as the 'rules' of social interactions are constantly changing depending on the age, environment, situation and gender of those involved. They have difficulty making and maintaining friendships and relationships, find it difficult to work in groups with peers and are particularly confused by unstructured times such as playtimes, lunchtimes and end of year 'off timetable' days.

It is true that there are differences in these three areas, but these do not have to be difficulties. They can cause difficulties, however, if there is not understanding on both sides and appropriate teaching, and if strategies are not in place, understood and used effectively over the long term.

It is important to remember that each child on the Autistic Spectrum is an individual. AS characteristics will present differently in each pupil and have varying impacts upon their ability to participate positively in school. Understanding and catering for a pupil's individual strengths and challenges is essential in order to support them to reach their fullest potential during their school years.

Autistic Spectrum characteristics impact on:

- potential strength areas, such as honesty or good memory;
- social interactions;
- communication;
- interests and behaviour, which may be restricted;
- sensory processing.

The following list shows likely indicators that a child may be on the Autistic Spectrum. Please remember, however, that only a qualified paediatrician can diagnose AS. The list here is intended to facilitate understanding of the range of complex behaviours that AS children may show.

If you teach a child for whom you would put 'yes when compared to the majority of children of the same age' beside most of the following statements, it would be wise to recommend that the parent/carer seeks further advice from their GP.

The targets listed in this book can support any child who shows the types of behaviours listed here, whether or not they have a diagnosis of AS.

	Yes/No
POTENTIAL STRENGTH AREAS	
Special interest area/s	
Long-term and accurate memory	
Liking for rules and sequences	
Visual thinking and learning	
Ability to decode text	
Reliability (maintains schedules and routines)	
Thinks in a precise and detailed way	
Literal, honest and direct	
Ability to focus (particularly for special interests)	

	Yes/No
SOCIAL INTERACTIONS	
Difficulty engaging in and maintaining typical social contact (including friendships)	
Lack of empathy (difficulty showing sensitivity to the feelings and needs of others)	
Difficulty reading and using facial expressions and body language	
Awareness of personal space (can have too little or be very aware)	
Difficulty with interpreting non-verbal language (for example, body language)	
Lack of or abnormal eye contact	
Difficulty with social interactions	
Lack of or difficulty in displaying affection	

	Yes/No
COMMUNICATION	
Comprehension of language lags behind expressive language	
Difficulty understanding non-verbal communication	
Difficulty with symbolic or abstract language (for example, idioms)	
Delays in speech acquisition	
Unusual speech patterns (for example, accent, rhythm, pitch, intonation)	
Echolalia (repetition of speech)	
Difficulties initiating and sustaining conversations	
Difficulty listening and following directions when they are given to whole class	

	Yes/No
RESTRICTED INTERESTS AND BEHAVIOUR	
May find surroundings confusing and unpredictable	
Difficulties 'making sense' of classroom and/or learning activities	
Changes in routines and/or environment may cause anger, fear, irritation and stress	
Obsessive behaviour in relation to interest, hobbies and objects	
Insistence on same and dislike of change	
Ritualistic behaviour (for example, taking same route to places)	
Lack of creativity and imagination	
May need help but doesn't know how to communicate need or who to go to for help	

	Yes/No
SENSORY PROCESSING	
Variable sensitivities depending upon situation and individual stress threshold	
Delayed reaction/response	
Anger, stress, or anxiety reactions	
Hearing (for example, makes sounds to screen out unwanted noise)	
Sight (for example, is sensitive to pulsations in lighting)	
Touch (for example, avoids touch or contact)	
Taste and smell (for example, dislikes strong smells such as perfume)	
Movement, balance, gravity (for example, seems oblivious to danger of heights)	
Movement, awareness of one's own position (for example, exerts too much pressure when handling objects)	
Taste (for example, eats only certain food)	

Implications for learners

The difficulties listed in the previous section mean that the experience of a school day is very different for children on the Autistic Spectrum compared to that of other pupils. The skills required cannot be placed into categories and applied when appropriate, as there is a great deal of overlapping. This also causes confusion for the AS child, as it is not possible to provide a 'recipe' to apply in certain situations.

Social and emotional factors

Empathy and trust are the basics for effective and constructive communication and the development of relationships. The AS child does not have the ability to copy or learn these skills without direct intervention and teaching. As the AS child matures, they become aware of friendships and may want to have them. However, they have difficulties in knowing how to interact and in understanding what is deemed appropriate. This is made more confusing for the AS child because social rules cannot be rote-learned, but have to be applied and modified according to the situation. The AS child may present as aloof and try to avoid other people, or may make approaches to other people in ways which are inappropriate or odd. AS children may show lack of awareness and understanding of other people's feelings, and may also have difficulty in recognising and expressing their own feelings.

In order to support the AS child through this process it is necessary to help them develop the following skills:

- sharing ideas and solutions;
- solving problems;
- communicating effectively;
- avoiding or defusing conflict.

Teaching these skills directly in groups, and giving the child an opportunity to practise them and hear feedback, will allow the AS child to build confidence in these areas.

Flexibility of thought/rigid thinking

The AS child has difficulty stopping and moving on from activities. In young children, the difficulties in flexible thinking are shown by a failure to play like other children. Some children may not develop any imaginative play at all, while others may copy play themes from other children or from stories or videos. A child in the playground may be able to join in a game about Harry Potter, but be unable to veer from the exact story line and go with the flow of the other children. This may also lead to difficulties coping with change, and the development of repetitive activities and fixed routines.

Language and communication

The difficulties in communication affect non-verbal communication (for example, tone of voice, facial expression, eye contact) as well as verbal communication. The AS child cannot 'read' these signals like the other children in the class. Language development may or may not be delayed, but AS children have a language disorder affecting the meanings of words and language. These difficulties may range from not understanding other people's communication at all, to more subtle difficulties such as literal interpretation of phrases such as 'raining cats and dogs'. The child may have acquired a very good vocabulary, but have little understanding of the real meaning, and so find the whole situation extremely confusing and sometimes frightening.

Difficulties also involve the social use of communication. These difficulties can cover a wide range, from functional communication of basic needs only, to problems when taking part in a conversation, such as not understanding or taking account of the needs of the other person.

Sensory differences

In addition, pupils with AS characteristics can often have sensory differences. This means that they may react to sensory stimulants very differently from other children. This may include being hypersensitive (showing increased sensitivity) or hyposensitive (showing reduced sensitivity).

This can have an impact on any of the senses, so AS children may have difficulties in the following areas:

- **Visual**: they may have strong likes/dislikes of colours, patterns and so on.
- **Auditory**: they may have an acute awareness of noise, which may even cause them pain.
- **Tactile**: they may find certain fabrics distressing, or be extremely concerned about keeping clean. Touch may cause pain, or they may have no reaction to pain.
- **Taste and smell**: they may only eat a limited selection of foods, and find certain smells offensive.
- **Vestibular**: they may enjoy and seek out sensations that challenge balance, with little perception of danger.
- **Proprioceptive and proxemic**: they may be unaware of personal boundaries, their position in space and so on.

Sensory difficulties will require careful consideration of the teaching and learning environment for difficulties presented. Parents and siblings are often a good source of information on specific intolerances. All AS children will be unique in the stimulants that they react to, so these will need to be observed and an appropriate response made.

The whole spectrum

The behaviours which are characteristic of the Autistic Spectrum are the outcome of differences in the ways that AS children think and experience the world. This makes the classroom and school a very confusing and challenging environment for them. The Autistic Spectrum can be likened to a rainbow. At different stages in the child's life they can be at different places on the rainbow, experiencing either a partial range of colours or the full spectrum.

Strategies for an AS-friendly classroom

The AS-friendly classroom is a learner-friendly classroom, since all learners will benefit from strategies put in place to support AS children. Different suggestions will be appropriate for different age groups and children. Some of the ideas will be appropriate for your situation, whereas there will be good reasons why others are less suitable for you. You should take from this list only what is relevant for the learners in your classroom and for you.

Social Stories™

The strategy of using Social Stories™ was first defined in 1991 by Carol Gray. Her website www.thegraycenter.org contains explanations, examples and details of training centres and courses, and resources are available for purchase. This strategy is suggested several times in this book.

Often social situations are unstructured, with no obvious rules. This means AS children do not know what to do or say and this makes them anxious or worried. Social Stories can be used across all age ranges and used to teach social understanding in a wide variety of situations. These might include how to wait in a queue, asking someone to play, self-care and personal skills and, later on in life, how to ask for a date or order food in a restaurant. This then teaches skills that many people accept as known, or think very little about, but which can be a confusing minefield for an AS child. A Social Story can provide the child with a kind of reassurance and much-needed structure, which makes them feel safe. The story is written from the perspective of the AS child. The rewards from this process are twofold: they are helpful for the child, but also the teacher writing the story develops a deeper insight into the world and different way of thinking experienced by the AS child.

- A Social Story is individualised and specific to the need of the child for whom it is written.
- The presentation of the materials can vary according to the needs of the individual, with more visuals if necessary, using photographs, signs or symbols.

Case study

A Year 2 child in school had a constantly running nose. The child was not aware that it was time to wipe or blow their nose. Other children and adults found the sight unpleasant. Telling the child to wipe their nose or doing it for them did not teach the independent skill required. However, a Social Story indicating when it was necessary for the child to wipe their nose and the step-by-step process to follow did teach these skills.

It will be necessary for the adult to support the child and revisit the Social Story on several occasions in order that the skill is learned. It may also be necessary to revisit Social Stories even after it is felt the skill is acquired, as a reminder. Some children like to revisit their folder of Social Stories in order to feel confident in what they have learned and judge their own progression in social skills.

Case study

A Year 5 child was worried about what it would be like when his new sibling was born. A Social Story helped to explain that the child would still be loved in the family because he himself was special. Another Social Story could prepare the child for changes that he might experience when the baby arrives.

Social Stories are frequently useful for the following purposes:

- To clarify expectations for following school rules. If a child has misunderstood a school rule (for example, they told the truth when a little diplomacy might have been more helpful) a Social Story can help to clarify the situation.
- To explain to children about behaviour expectations in unfamiliar places, for example, when going on a school trip or going swimming.
- To warn children about a change in routine, for example, a theatre company coming into school or a different adult in the classroom.
- To prepare older children for the unknown factors of changes due to puberty. These are hard enough to cope with for young people without Autistic Spectrum characteristics and are frequently very challenging to those with a diagnosis, who do not understand what is happening to them.
- To teach children how to understand commonly used idioms and phrases. The literal-thinking AS child may not interpret idioms such as 'Hang on' or 'We've run out of glue sticks' in the way the teacher intended, and be confused.

The inclusion of choices in the Social Story format is very helpful in encouraging the child to follow the path of making the right choice and being rewarded for this, rather than making the wrong choice, to which there is a consequence.

An example of a Social Story for a child who greets people and doesn't know when to stop might be:

Saying hello and goodbye
My name is Jo and I live in Cambridge.
I go to Green Primary School.

When people meet they usually say hello once.
I will try to say hello once.
I will try to say hello once and walk away.
It is good to say hello once.

When people go away they say goodbye once.
I will try to say goodbye once.
I will try to say goodbye once and walk away.
It is good to say goodbye once and walk away.

More advice on writing Social Stories is available in *The New Social Story Book* by Carol Gray (Future Horizons Inc, 2010, with CD), and Carol Gray's updated guidelines can be purchased and downloaded in pdf form from www.thegraycenter.org.

Break systems

A formalised break or time out system is a helpful strategy in the classroom, allowing children to have a sensory break and then re-engage and re-access the cognitive process.

Children are provided with a visual representation of the number of breaks, with the time and place designated. Generally a child can take up to six 5- to 10-minute breaks each day. They are not allowed to take more than six, but can take fewer. A designated break area in the classroom is set up; this can be as simple as a bean bag in a corner, the book corner, or a den or pop-up tent such as a dark den. A timer is used in order that the beginning and end of the break is defined. The child can take another break immediately after the first one, but must consider that their limit is six a day. The emphasis is that the break is a sensory break or calm-down time, and the child must re-engage with the learning task. It is not a get-out-of-work-free system!

Comic strip conversations

Comic strip conversations are a technique developed by Carol Gray (*Comic Strip Conversations*, Future Horizons, 1994). This is a tool to support and aid AS children in their understanding of communication.

A series of pictures and symbols are used for different aspects of conversation and colours can be used to indicate feelings. It is represented as a conversation between two people, using stick people and speech and thought bubbles. These enable the child to read things into conversations that they may not have been aware of previously.

Drawings are annotated and speech bubbles can be drawn in different ways to indicate feelings. They are helpful in developing an understanding of theory of mind (see page 38), and discovering that not all children think in the same way and that others may be experiencing different feelings.

It is not necessary for the adult to be good at drawing, or artistic, as this is a simple visual representation rather than an artist's impression. In fact, as the child becomes more familiar with using the strategy, it is more likely that they will draw themselves. This is good, as they begin to take ownership of the situation and take responsibility for the learning. Children have an interest in the technique and can access it easily as it is broken down into manageable chunks.

Comic strip conversations are useful for practising social skills or conversations in preparation for an event: for example, if a visitor is expected in school and greetings will need to be made. They are also helpful when revisiting situations and considering the choices made and whether a different choice could have been made.

Fig. 5: An example of a comic strip conversation.

Colours are used on the drawing to indicate the feelings of the character. The children are encouraged to annotate using colours, and appropriate colours for each emotion are suggested. For example, red for anger, blue for sadness (see Carol Gray, *Comic Strip Conversations*).

It is helpful to set up scenarios to practise using the colours and to develop understanding. For example, it could feature an angry and anxious character and a discussion could follow about how the character shows their feelings. Reference is made to their body language and facial expression, but also to their thoughts.

'Circle of Friends'

The 'Circle of Friends' is a peer-based approach to supporting children with Autistic Spectrum characteristics in school. It originated in North America as one of a range of strategies to promote the inclusion into mainstream schools of students with disabilities and difficulties.

A Circle of Friends is a group of children who volunteer to provide support and feedback to the child with AS (the 'focus child'). Together, they try to create practical solutions to problems in school (ranging from relationships with others, to temper tantrums, to making wrong choices, to unwillingness to begin work, to any other difficulty the AS child faces) and support the focus child in implementing the plans. In addition, the Circle of Friends provides supportive comments to encourage the focus child when they have made good choices and put aspects of the agreed solution into place.

Setting up a 'Circle of Friends'

When a Circle is established, a group of six to eight volunteers meets regularly with the focus child and an adult facilitator. The Circle acts as a resource to suggest strategies and set targets to deal with difficulties that have been jointly identified by the members of the Circle and the focus child.

In setting up a Circle of Friends there are a number of stages:

- explaining about Circle of Friends and getting permission for involvement from school staff, parents and the focus child;
- talking to the whole class or tutor group to recruit volunteers;
- starting and continuing with the Circle.

Parents need to know clearly what is entailed and must be given some realistic idea of possible outcomes. In this respect the term 'Circle of Friends' is rather misleading in implying that friendships can be created simply by seeking volunteers in this fashion. It is important to make this clear.

Remember that a Circle can only be set up and run with the free and informed consent of the focus child.

Finding the volunteers

One way to find volunteers is to give the whole class slips of paper and ask them to write their name on this with a 'yes' if they are interested in volunteering, or a 'no' if they are not. This can happen at the end of a whole-class talk and catch the enthusiasm built up during the session. It can be explained, at this point, that there may be too many volunteers, as only six or eight are required, but that those who were not initially involved could be placed on a reserve list. It can also be stressed that if a volunteer decides they do not wish to continue being a member of the Circle then they can easily leave.

Case study

A teacher gave a Year 3 child the target to *improve social interactions in the playground*. A discussion with the teacher, exploring the child's strengths and weaknesses, revealed that the main problem was that the child did not join in with a group in the playground, but remained on the periphery watching. He struggled to know how to join in and understand the games the other children played, and so watched them in the hope of learning what was going on. This was what the teacher had noticed, but the target *to improve social interactions in the playground* did not accurately pinpoint anything that was useful to the child. The target was too large and therefore it was too much for the child to manage, and too difficult for the teacher and SENCo to monitor progression. Breaking this down in to an achievable 'small-step' target was more meaningful and useful for all involved. Using a 'Circle of Friends' approach gave this child security in the playground, guidance and a support group on which to build his social interactions.

Managing challenging behaviours

When a child is proving to be very challenging, it is difficult for the adults and other children too. The best strategy is to try to avoid unwanted behaviours.

- Set basic ground rules, which are consistently adhered to in the classroom, playground and any environment the child will access. This provides clear and consistent boundaries.

- Make positive references to the children who are modelling the right choice of behaviour in order to reinforce the expectations of the classroom and school.

- Reiterate the rules frequently and do not assume that the AS child will be remembering them because the other children can. It may be necessary to support these rules with visuals and spend time talking about them regularly. Statements of reality are helpful in focusing the child on the appropriate behaviours being demonstrated, for example, '*Look, Thomas is standing in the line looking at Mrs Smith. What do you think you should do?*'

- Explain and reinforce any non-verbal communication. '*Mrs Smith has her arms folded; do you think she is happy with the noise the children are making in the hall? What do you think you should do?*'

- Assess the mood in which the child has arrived at school or the lesson. Know your child. If they are not in the frame of mind to access learning immediately, set up 'meet and greet' at the beginning of the day or after lunchtime and complete a calming activity or talk time prior to beginning the classroom task.

- Act as you say you will. Do not make promises and then change them. The AS child may view this as telling lies, unless an explanation is given, and will lose trust. For example, '*I am sorry, I thought that we were going to carry on with the History work about the Tudors today, but the computers are being used by another class so we are going to do this instead.*'

- Avoid shouting and physical contact. Try to keep your voice slow and calm; if you raise your voice you are modelling to the child a behaviour that is inappropriate. The AS child may also believe this is being aimed directly at them. This can also occur when the behaviour is directed at others.

- Use visual prompts to remind about choices and appropriate behaviours.

- Use the school reward system where appropriate, but if necessary encourage the child to engage by using their special interest as a reward. For example, '*Three sentences of writing then you can look at your special book for 3 minutes using a timer*'. Then three more sentences, and so on. Or have reward systems where minutes are earned in golden time on their chosen activity, for example, the Lego® box. Be careful to make the activity one which can be managed in the school environment, not something that will disrupt the learning of other pupils and cause conflict among peers.

- Share, talk and problem-solve with parents and all other adults who have contact with the child in school, principally other teachers, TAs and lunchtime supervisors. Focus on the positive behaviours and how to encourage these.
- Set clear consequences for inappropriate and unwanted behaviours. Consequences are important to teach the child what is inappropriate; these help the child to learn and move them forwards.
- Avoid sarcasm. The AS child will not understand this and will interpret it literally.
- Look for and reward the positives at all times, whether with a comment, a smile, a thumbs up or a larger reward.
- Set up a positive communication book between home and school which records only positive behaviours to be celebrated, no matter how small. Include written comments, photographs and copies of pieces of work. Encourage parents to reciprocate with positive behaviours from home to be celebrated in school. For example, '*Alice helped to clear away her toys before dinner; good choice Alice*'.

However hard you work to maintain a calm and consistent classroom, many AS children will have days or times when they cannot cope and their behaviour escalates. If this happens, bear in mind the following guidelines.

- Try to consider the issues which are causing the challenging behaviour and do not take it personally.
- Try to remain calm yourself in the situation, and avoid engaging in confrontation. This makes it more difficult for all involved.
- Avoid losing control yourself. Keep your emotions neutral. If you feel that your emotions are being compromised, and you are feeling stressed, allow another adult to take over the situation and move away to calm down.
- If the child is further away, for example, in the playground, and you need to engage with them, move slowly towards them in order that you can be heard without using a loud voice; the AS child may feel that if your voice is raised you are shouting at them. If necessary move to the side of the child so that you are not viewed as being confrontational and aggressive by invading their personal space.
- Explain the situation and encourage the child to make the right choice.
- If the child is safe, move away in order that they can make this choice independently. Prompt, but do not nag!
- Allow the child time to calm down without further stimulus, be this talking, proximity or even looking towards them.
- Do not expect the child to be able to explain what the problem is there and then, even if the child appears to have calmed. Any further stimulus can heighten the situation again and cause a further outburst.
- Explain that it is the behaviour, not the child, that you do not like.

- Allow the child to express their view when calm. Listen and acknowledge what the child has said, then explain why it is possible to meet the child's expectation, or why it is not possible.
- Record the times and types of behaviours and look for triggers. You may find that all the problems occur during the same lesson and the problem is around self-esteem or limited understanding of the language being used.
- Refocus the child as quickly as possible on the activity following a break, discussion or time out. The behaviour does not prevent the task from being completed; the child always has to return to the task set by the adult. The AS child may otherwise learn that the behaviour means that the activity can be avoided, and may repeat the behaviour.
- Avoid asking questions such as, *'Why did you do that?'* The AS child will not know why. Instead ask, *'What do you think you should have done?'* or *'How could you have made a better choice?'* A board like the one shown in Fig. 6 can be useful in structuring conversations.

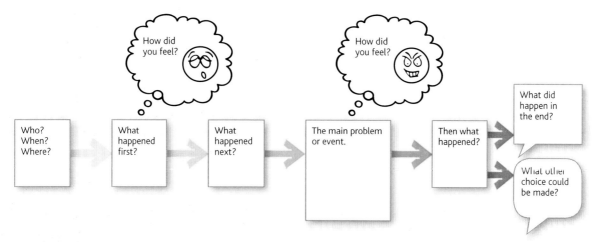

Fig. 6: A structure for revisiting and talking about an incident may help to focus the child and allow them to stick to the facts. You can use drawings or words to aid the explanations in the boxes, or use them as a structure for talking, in order to move the narrative forwards.

Structuring tasks

Children with Autistic Spectrum characteristics respond well to structure. This makes things predictable for them and reduces stress and confusion; it also supports the child's strengths in their liking of routine and repetition. Structure also helps them to develop independent strategies.

However, it is vital that in the very early stages the child is exposed to and learns about change. We are unable to predict and structure everything about the school day for them, but we are able to understand and accommodate this need.

Personal space

AS children may be easily distracted and may need a personal space to work; this may be called a workstation or 'Joe's table' and should have all the necessary equipment to hand in order that tasks can be completed more easily. The child's desire to finish can be used to the teacher's and teaching assistant's advantage in the classroom. As the child becomes older they will want to work alongside their peers on a table and small adaptations can help the child to understand the limits of their working environment. For example, you may like to stick a piece of coloured tape on the table top to denote personal working space, or – if the child moves classrooms for different lessons – a ruler, book or pencil case can denote the limits of their area. This gives a physical boundary for the child to work within and means they do not encroach on the work space of peers or vice versa.

During circle time, denoting a 'carpet place' is helpful. This can be a certain picture on the carpet, for example, *'Your sitting place is on the leaf with C on it'*, or a carpet square or cushion. This can then be moved to the hall or other classrooms and denotes the child's individual space.

Visual timetables

A timetable helps the child to understand what is going to happen throughout the morning, afternoon or whole day, depending on what the individual child can manage. If there is a change to the routine or timetable, prepare the child for this so that it does not come as a shock, as they may react negatively to this. Preparations can take the form of a discussion or photos or symbols explaining the change. For example, *'The weather is too wet for us to go on the field for PE today because the children may slip and hurt themselves and this would not be safe so we are going to do PE in the hall. This may mean that the activities we will have to do will be different too.'* You may then wish to show the child a photograph of a PE lesson in the hall to remind them, or take them to see the hall prior to the activity.

With small children, the timetable can take the form of Now and Next symbols or photographs. As the child becomes older you can create a visual timetable using symbols for tasks and, later on, written words. Some children may like to cross out or remove the symbols to show that the task has been completed; this gives them an indication that time is progressing and that they are completing the day's activities, and so promotes success.

Structuring activities within the school day

Younger children respond well to a box or basket system in which daily 'must do' activities are placed. This is based on the principle of TEACCH™, developed in North Carolina, USA: see www.teacch.com. The boxes or baskets can be placed on the child's work space or alongside peers. The task is placed in one box and the reward in the next box. The task must be completed before the reward. You may wish to add Now and Next symbols to the boxes, or colour code them. Initially with support, the child learns to work through a series of adult-directed activities and is rewarded following these. Ultimately the child learns the system and is able to complete the tasks independently. At the start, tasks are small and well within the child's ability in order to learn the technique and a reward is quickly provided to motivate further involvement. Gradually tasks are built up in difficulty, extended by time or extended by number so two or three activities must be completed in order to gain the reward. It may be helpful to introduce an 'I am working for' chart at this stage. In order to gain the reward the child must complete several activities and gain three stars or stickers to exchange for the reward. This will help to increase their independent learning strategies.

As the child becomes older, breaking down tasks using a schedule or task card may be helpful. These can be produced on a small whiteboard or notebook. They may help to plan and structure the work, enabling the child to see the progression they are making towards the end of the task. They also help with starting tasks and making the task seem more manageable and possible. They can take the form of a table, chart or tick list. For example, when writing an explanation text, a paragraph plan with key words will help to guide the child through the task. Allocating an area of the classroom where finished work is placed is also helpful.

A well-organised classroom, with good practice in place, is of benefit to all children, not just those on the AS spectrum.

AS children and language

Children with Autistic Spectrum characteristics can have variable difficulties with speech and language. These can include problems with word and sentence meaning, intonation and rhythm. These difficulties interfere with the child's ability to interact with and interpret the world around them, be that the playground, classroom, dining hall, swimming pool or a school visit to the zoo. Some experts associate this difficulty with 'theory of mind', the ability to imagine the thoughts of others or put themselves in 'someone else's shoes'.

> Theory of mind is important because 'the ability to make inferences about what other people believe to be the case in a given situation allows one to predict what they will do'.
>
> (S. Baron-Cohen, A.M. Leslie and U. Frith, 1985, 'Does the autistic child have a "theory of mind"?', *Cognition*, 21, 37–46)

A simple test called the 'Sally Anne Test' was developed in 1985 by psychologists Simon Baron-Cohen, Alan Leslie and Uta Frith to indicate whether a child has developed the ability to understand their own and other people's beliefs, desires, intentions and emotions.

The Sally Anne test

To start the test, have two figures/children (Sally and Anne) and introduce them to the child. *'This is Sally. This is Anne.'*

Begin to set up the scenario as follows by telling the story. *'Sally has a red box with a lid and Anne has a blue bag, which has a zip.'* Show these items to the child.

Place the box and bag in front of the appropriate figure.

'Sally and Anne have been playing with a ball.' Demonstrate this with the figures and the ball. *'Sally feels thirsty and puts the ball in the red box and closes the lid.'* Demonstrate this with the ball and close the lid of the box so it is no longer visible. *'Sally goes inside to get a drink where she can no longer see the box.'*

'While she is out of sight Anne moves the ball from the red box to the blue bag and closes the zip.' Show this to the child and leave the ball in the bag and close the zip.

'Sally returns, having had her drink.'

Now ask the child the following questions: *'Which one is Sally?' 'Which one is Anne?' 'Where is the ball now?' 'Where did Sally put the ball?'*

Now the theory of mind question.

- *'When she comes back, where will Sally look for the ball?'*

If the child realises that Sally will look for the ball in the red box and not in the blue bag where Anne moved it to, then the child can understand Sally's perspective and has theory of mind. Sally will believe the ball is where she left it because she was out of the room when Anne moved the ball.

If the child says that Sally will look for the ball in Anne's bag then you *might* say the child does not have theory of mind. In this case the child does not appear to understand Sally's perspective – that Sally did not see Anne take the ball from the box and put it in the bag.

You can adapt the test to suit the child's preferences. For example, two boys could be playing football, the characters could be adults, or the whole test can be acted out by adults.

The evidence suggests that some AS children have little ability to understand theory of mind and so we have to teach this. An understanding of whether the child can understand the thinking of others is of great help to us when discussing situations with the child and rebuilding issues.

Language and talk for learning in the classroom

Considering why some things are difficult to understand for the AS child will help us to adapt our language and teaching and improve learning for the child. The following factors may make the language we use difficult to understand:

- jargon and technical words;
- long words;
- unfamiliar vocabulary;
- idioms;
- flat or sarcastic intonation;
- complex and long sentences;
- words out of context;
- lack of visual support;
- external distractions (noise, interruptions and so on);
- internal factors (how the child feels and what is on their mind).

It is not necessary to avoid such elements of language completely, but it is important to consider the different way of thinking of the AS child and include explanations where possible.

You can support the AS child's access to the learning in the classroom by using some of the techniques indicated in Fig. 7.

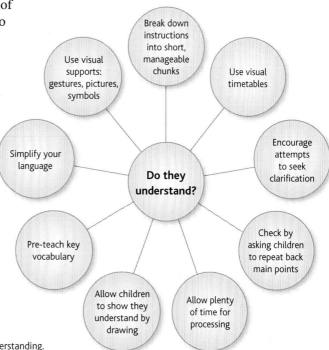

Fig. 7: Strategies for improving understanding.

The Target Ladders

Letter	Being with others	Coping with rules and change of rules	Sharing friends	Empathy
A	Indicates like/dislike by gesture	Follows simple request of adult (e.g. places shape in box)	Identifies/recognises friend	Shows awareness of others
A	Anticipates by indicating (e.g. points to cup for drink)	Follows request of adult repetitively with slight adaptation (e.g. places two shapes in box, varies order)		Accepts and is comforted by some appropriate physical contact
B	Recognises familiar adults; indicates recognition by repeated movement, noise, facial expression	Watches and adapts – anticipates action, but willing to change	Allows one other to play alongside self and friend without interaction	Shows awareness of peers at play activities
B	Responds to familiar adults – turns to voice	Attempts untried activity (e.g. page turning in a different book)	Allows one other to play alongside self and friend. Interacts with other	Watches others engaged in activities
C	Shows an adult what they want to do	Spends 5 minutes alone at a self-chosen activity	Plays with friend in a small group without interaction	Attempts to negotiate with others (e.g. swap a toy, indicate turn)
C	Indicates a simple need	Self-directs to new task and chooses appropriate resources (e.g. chooses paper and finds pencil to draw)	Plays with friend in a small group with interaction	Recognises that others may be involved in group activities
D	Plays alone in own space	Follows peers' requests – copies repetitive play	Plays alongside friend who interacts with others (turn-taking) repetitively	Involved in exchange of ideas and information
D	Plays alone in shared space	Makes requests of peers – repetitive play	Plays alongside friend, engaged in play with other involving talk	

Suggested activities or strategies

Note: It is important to realise that in general children on the Autistic Spectrum do not learn by observation and need to have skills directly taught and modelled. However, all AS children are individuals and needs may differ for each child.

Sharing with others

- Use photographs of family members and friends to secure recognition of familiar people. Ask the child to identify a known person from a choice of two photographs (for example, '*Which one is Mrs Green?*') and then build up to three or four.
- Give the child and a friend a simple activity, for example pushing cars down a ramp, finding toys in the sand, pouring from one container into others. Develop the activity to include, for example, pouring water into a second container. Water or sand toys that spin or turn a wheel are useful at this stage.
- Give a pair of children a large box of toys to share.
  - Set up opportunities where one additional child joins the pair and accesses the toys.
  - Use verbal prompts to indicate that this is an appropriate way to play and is the beginning of sharing and turn-taking.
- Congratulate and reward the child for co-operating and allowing others to use the same resources. Use direct, simple language, for example '*Good sharing*'. Ensure you identify the skill that has been performed well rather than saying, '*Good girl, good boy*'.

Taking turns

Set up opportunities for turn-taking activities. Initially these are adult-led; you and the child take turns.

- Encourage another child to join in. It is useful to have two toys; for example, when pouring sand have one object to pour into, but two to pour from. This enables the initial teaching of turn-taking without the AS child feeling the anxiety of losing the toy to another child.
- Once this is established, initiate turn-taking and waiting with a peer. It may be necessary to use a visual prompt or hand signal to indicate waiting at first. A visual timer (sand/timer type) is also useful in these initial learning stages.

Modelling appropriate language

'*Whose turn is it?*' '*Whose turn is it to wait?*' At this stage allow the children to become involved in the language, but beware of one child being over-assertive or beginning to dictate.

- Introduce simple board games. Initially, play alone with the child, but gradually allow one or two other children to join you. Constantly use the language of turn-taking and sharing.
- Encourage the child to watch peers playing. Verbalise what you see, for example, '*Look, good turn-taking*', '*Good waiting*'. Explain why this is a good choice. In general AS children need to have skills directly taught and modelled. A running commentary by the adult will help the child to observe peers and recognise the good choices they are making.

Letter	Being with others	Coping with rules and change of rules	Sharing friends	Empathy
E	Plays alongside others and can watch them	Takes part in familiar activities with peers (e.g. clapping games, songs with actions)	Plays separately from friend, who plays elsewhere in classroom	Can make suggestions about the roles of others in an activity
E	Plays alongside and engages in simple sharing, with support	Communicates to peer what is needed for activity	Plays (outdoors) separately from friend who plays elsewhere in playground	Adapts ideas and suggestions in response to others' views in an activity
F	Plays alongside and engages in simple sharing, without support	Works in small group to gather items for familiar game	Has more than one friend – recognises things in common with each one	Asks others if they like an activity
F	Plays in a pair. Will do things others have done for them (e.g. roll ball back)	Talks about what is needed for a familiar game with small group	Recognises likes and dislikes in others	Asks others if they want to take part in an activity
G	Will engage in play with a partner (e.g. cooking in home corner)	Talks about what is needed for unfamiliar game with small group	Recognises others have more than one friend based on common interests	Understands others may want to take different roles in an activity
G	Will engage in play with more than one peer		Accepts peers may have more than one friend, which may vary	Accepts others may not want to take part in an activity
H	Takes turns independently (e.g. pushing car down ramp)	Can play unfamiliar game with small group	Allows friends to play together without interruption	Recognises when others are unhappy or upset
H	Leads, follows or starts play	Willingly joins in familiar games with familiar rules	Offers assistance when friend needs help (not all the time)	Offers appropriate verbal response to comfort others

Suggested activities or strategies

Sharing with one child

- Create a rule that everyone has to experience being the leader and also being last in the line when lining up for PE, assembly, lunchtime and so on. Allocate the child a regular place in the line, for example number 3, which they have unless it is their turn to be leader. (It is advisable that this place is not the first or last, as this can create problems with peers.) Prepare the child for this role and the roles of others before the line moves forwards.
- Give opportunities for the child to wait their turn in appropriate play and encourage them to watch their peers enjoying the toys.
- Model conversation with peers – '*Have you finished? It's my turn now*'. Encourage waiting for a response time.
- Set up activities that need two or three parts, for example the cars and the ramp in different boxes. Encourage the child and a peer to collect the parts separately and set up the activity together.
- Set up activities in PE to share equipment for balancing and walking and for rolling, balancing or kicking a ball.

Sharing with more than one child

Once the child is turn-taking consistently with a familiar peer, introduce a second peer. Give opportunities for all three children to take part in the turn-taking and playing activities.

- Introduce games of Follow the Leader and vary who plays the leader. These can be physical games, such as skipping, jumping or rolling, or (in the classroom) copying the way a toy moves with another toy, for example making a bear jump then making a car do it in the same way. Alternatively, play in the home corner by stirring a pan and then copying.
- Give opportunities for the two peers to play together in order that the child does not come to expect that they can control one friend, and begins to understand that friends have other friends too.

- Introduce activities involving feelings visuals. Introduce photographs of a child who is crying, jumping for joy and so on. Look at the photo and, in the little groups, discuss how the child in the photo is feeling and what we can see that tells us this. Begin to investigate why the feeling may have occurred. For example, '*Do you think the girl may be crying because the boy has taken her toy from her? Do you think she feels sad about this?*' '*Do you think the boy is happy to be receiving a present? How does his face tell us he is happy?*' Once the children are familiar with the visuals, use the photographs to play games such as Lotto, Snap or memory games.

Communicating with others

Introduce new games or activities with small groups.

- Model comfort and verbal responses and acknowledge them verbally in other children.
- Identify and point out appropriate responses to the AS child. Be very specific.
- Make use of feelings visuals to identify and communicate feelings in self and others. Point to cartoon or actual faces to identify their feelings. Acknowledge by saying '*Thank you for showing me*'. In this way you are beginning the communication process and establishing an understanding of how feelings affect them.
- Build in opportunities to talk after the feelings visual, accompanied by appropriate questions, for example, '*How did you feel when you won/lost?*' Teach that it is OK to feel upset or cross about not winning, but there are ways to react appropriately. In this way you are beginning to separate the feeling from the behaviour and teach appropriate and acceptable choices.

Letter	Being with others	Coping with rules and change of rules	Sharing friends	Empathy
I	Makes choices based on own interests	Can work with peers to plan adaptations to familiar games	Avoids 'shadowing' friends, as it makes them feel uncomfortable	Offers appropriate physical contact for others to comfort
I	Takes part in group activity and comments with adult support	Makes adaptations to familiar games and suggests these to peers	Shows restraint in regularity of contact	Seeks appropriate adult for support for others
J	Can ask others to join them in a game	Suggests adaptations to unfamiliar games with peers	Is able to control attention given to friend – so as not to appear obsessive and scare friend	Listens to views of others and make appropriate verbal response
J	Can talk about what 'fair' means	Can plan ahead a game to play next time	Understands that friend's preferences may change over time	Offers support and encouragement verbally to others
K	Can allow others to make changes and acknowledge fairness	Takes part in trial and error	Listens to a friend without being nosey or pushy	Accepts that others sometimes need to calm down
K	Acts as an equal in a group	Plays with 'non-friends' and adapts to 'new person' rules	Shows appropriate generosity without trying to 'buy' friendship	Makes suggestions to others to see opposing viewpoints
L	Can identify peers who have similar interests	Can remain emotionally calm and talk about 'new person' rules	Is protective of friends (reasonably), but not possessive	Accepts that peers sometimes have different views
L	Can sometimes consider other group members	Is able to respond to rule changes with appropriate language	Understands friendship is reciprocal; that is, one person isn't doing all the giving	Can sometimes accept things not happening as expected

Suggested activities or strategies

Understanding points of view

- Use familiar stories to explore the idea of viewpoint: how did the giant's wife feel at the end of Jack and the Beanstalk? How did all the other characters feel? How did Goldilocks feel at the end of her story? How did the bears feel?
- Create formal teaching opportunities using visual resources, for example comic strips, DVDs or SEAL (Social and Emotional Aspects of Learning) resources.
- Lead discussion in small groups about how viewpoints differ.
- Acknowledge the difficulties involved in accepting alternative views and give suggestions for appropriate phrases and language to be used in responses.

Following rules

- Have consistent and clear rules and boundaries – be explicit about these.
- Use direct explicit modelling of the rules for learning in your classroom, for example, listening.
- It may be helpful to have visual prompts in order to remind about the rules. This prevents 'nagging' and also does not disrupt other teaching and learning. It encourages decision-making and independent strategies, rather than over-reliance on an adult.
- Value special interests and where possible use them to reward. For example, if a child enjoys animal pictures, allow time to look at books as a reward.
- Always time the rewards in order that the adult remains calmly in control. Rewards can be actual objects, toys, photos, stickers …
- Use direct, simple language to prepare the child before something happens. For example, *'When we have walked to the hall you are going to sit at the front on your mat and wait quietly'*.
- During the compliant stage give constant, consistent verbal prompts, such as, *'Good sitting'*.

Expressing feelings appropriately: the Four Point Plan

There are four main steps to expressing feelings effectively and appropriately.

1 Recognise the feeling.
2 Stop and think about it.
3 Use 'I' statements to say what you think. For example, *'I don't like that'*, *'I am going to walk away'*, *'I need help'*.
4 Show respect for the other person.

Discussing examples of real-life situations can help children identify the feelings they experienced, the choices they made and the consequences of these. You can relate the discussion back to the Four Point Plan. For example:

What was the situation? *'My Mum asked me to tidy my bedroom when I had planned to meet my friends.'*

What did you think? *'She's mean; this is unfair; she hates my friends.'*

What did you feel? *'Angry.'*

What did you do? *'I shouted at my Mum and slammed the door.'*

What were the consequences? *'I got grounded and couldn't see my friends for a week.'*

Ask the child to consider how the Four Point Plan could have helped.

'I knew I was angry. I didn't stop and think and I made the wrong choice. I could have told my Mum how I felt then I wouldn't have been grounded.'

Letter	Being with others	Coping with rules and change of rules	Sharing friends	Empathy
M	Engages new group members in a game	Understands and adapts to flexibility in rules in varying social situations	Can 'take a break' from friends	Accepts another's point of view and accepts compromise
M	Co-operates with 'non-friends'	Is beginning to accept winning with appropriate reactions and language choices	Modifies and adapts reactions to a range of friends	Treats others as equals and does not intimidate or threaten
N	Identifies people who have negative influence on self and others	Accepts losing with appropriate reactions and language choices most of the time	Understands and accepts views of friends	Respects views or rights of others
N	Accepts that sometimes you may win and at other times may lose	Is willing to play again after defeat	Shows respect for views of friends	Respects others and uses appropriate language

The Target Ladders

Suggested activities or strategies

Social skills groups

It is important to include good role models in social skills groups and to be explicit about the skills being taught. It is also important to explain that peers 'may' react one way and to begin to teach that we cannot always predict the same reaction from another person.

- Set up opportunities in small groups of familiar peers and adults, where children feel comfortable, for children to air their views without judgement. For example, have a discussion on winning and losing, and learning the appropriate responses; a Social Story™ would also be useful.
- In a practical situation, being reminded or prompted beforehand of the appropriate response for winning and losing is useful. Give verbal praise for any appropriate responses that are made.
- Discuss appropriate language. Show that language choices vary according to the situation and the people present. Less formal, more colloquial language may be used appropriately when playing with friends but not in a school assembly or when having lunch with grandparents.

Circle of Friends

The aims of a Circle of Friends are:

- to create a support network for the AS child;
- to provide the child with encouragement and recognition for any achievements and progress;
- to work with the child to identify difficulties and devise practical ideas to help deal with these difficulties;
- to help to put these ideas into practice.

These strategies also include good peer role models. See page 31 for more details of the Circle of Friends approach.

Comic strip conversations

Comic strip conversations are conversations between two or more people, which incorporate the use of simple line drawings (see p. 30), providing additional support to individuals who struggle to comprehend the quick exchange of verbal information that occurs in a conversation. They can be used to:

- revisit or report back an incident;
- describe what is happening at the moment;
- plan and prepare for what may happen;
- explore emotions and feelings about situations.

Comic strip conversations identify what people say and do and what people may be thinking and feeling. They can give an insight into a child's perception and highlight any misunderstandings. The adult does not need to be good at drawing, in fact the poorer the adult is the more likely the child is to take over the pen and thereby ownership of the exercise.

Letter	What can I say? To whom and when?	Peer pressure	Growing up
A	Can say hello to familiar adults and family on meeting	Chooses to play alongside	Reacts to parents when they come into school
A	Can say or gesture goodbye to familiar adults and family on leaving	Can politely refuse an offer from others to play	Can identify close family members
B	Can say or gesture hello and goodbye to peers	Can express dislike to others appropriately	Can identify boys and girls
B		Can indicate a desire to play	
C	Makes simple statements (e.g. 'I want ...') to peers in wider school community	Leads play with peers	Can identify an image of a boy's or girl's body unclothed
C	Responds to unfamiliar adults (in safe environments)	Does not always need to lead play	
D	Asks simple social questions of peers (e.g. 'My name is ... what is yours?')	Can make own choice, differing from peers (e.g. choose different food)	Knows own gender
D	Makes simple social requests to peers (e.g. 'Would you like to play?')		Matches own sex to picture of unclothed boy or girl

Suggested activities or strategies

Asking for things

Use free play to identify opportunities to teach the child about requesting interactions with other children. For example, if the child is watching a group playing with bikes in a racing game from the periphery, talk to the child and identify whether they are happy to watch or would like to join in with their peers' play. Give the child words they can use and show them how to approach another child and make this request. Model this behaviour and allow the peer to respond. Give examples of a variety of responses and explain their meaning. For example, a peer may respond, '*OK, when I get to the bridge*', '*You have the red bike*', '*You will have to wait*'. Show the child what to do next. Do not expect that the child will generalise this skill. Just because you have taught them how to do this with the bike, do not expect them to be able to do it when it comes to building a robot in the classroom. The AS child will need to have the skill taught as a new situation. You may need to go though the whole process several times in a variety of situations.

- Role-play activities with toys, modelling social interactions. In that way you can use toys to practise the skills outlined above. For example: '*Bear and Pig are playing football. Dog is watching. What could Dog say to Pig if he wanted to join in? Show me what he would do and what he would say.*'

Introducing gender

- Do sorting activities with pictures of girls and boys. Use photographs of peers in school uniform and organise them in groups, or post them into post boxes. Look carefully at the parts of the body that at this stage denote gender, as it is not always possible to use clothing for this purpose, especially during the winter when both girls and boys often wear trousers and the regulation school sweatshirt. Identify the fact that girls' hair may be long and tied up or they may wear hair accessories. Boys may also have long hair but usually loose, without accessories.
- Ask children to line up according to gender; this can be a warm-up game in PE lessons or when leaving the classroom or playground. Point out to the AS child who are the girls and who are the boys in the line.
- Further activities could involve using toys and small world characters, sorting boys and girls according to their clothing and hair, pretending to do 'lining up the class in girls and boys', and so on.

Using appropriate talk

- Model opportunities in both formal and informal situations. Set up opportunities in school for greetings; ensure that all adults, when passing, greet the child and wait for a response. Make sure that the adult has time to await the response, and if this is not the case, then do not initiate the greeting. Use a variety of words meaning the same: for example, '*Hello, Hi*' and colloquial greetings such as '*Watcha*'.
- During free play observe the child closely and use opportunities to model appropriate talk such as, '*Can I help you?*' or '*Can I have a go with the car?*' Act on opportunities as they arise, demonstrating and then giving the child an opportunity to practise, with prompting and support, in a comfortable environment and situation. Be vigilant and observant, looking for learning opportunities at all times to demonstrate interactions to the child. Use peers where appropriate to model appropriate skills; identify situations that occur naturally and direct the child to observe and copy the other child. Make opportunities for repetitive and frequent practice in free play situations.

Making independent choices

Provide a choice of two different activities for the child and a peer. Prepare the child by stating that either choice is correct. Once the child is able to choose, include choices for more formal learning tasks; for example, '*You can sit here or there*' or '*You can do this first or second*'. Gradually extend the choice of activities – perhaps using a choice board – until the child is able to take part in free choosing.

Letter	What can I say? To whom and when?	Peer pressure	Growing up
E	Asks questions for support (e.g. '*Can you help me?*') with peers and familiar adults	Acts as an equal member of a group	Can identify a man and a woman
E	Asks questions offering support (e.g. '*Can I help you?*') with peers and familiar adults	Is not dominated or intimidated	
F	Asks questions which may elicit varying responses (e.g. '*Can we share? Can I join in?*') with peers and familiar adults	Appropriately communicates dissatisfaction to an adult	Talks about what they did as a baby
F		Appropriately communicates dissatisfaction to a peer	Knows that they will be a man or woman
G	Makes suggestions which may elicit varying responses (e.g. '*Shall we do it this way?*') with peers and familiar adults	Identifies others who seek attention by inappropriate means	Uses appropriate toilet in familiar surroundings
G	Asks questions (e.g. '*Is that OK with you?*') of peers and familiar adults	Avoids others who seek attention by inappropriate means	Identifies appropriate toilet in unfamiliar surroundings
H	Makes statements of preferred option (e.g. '*I want ...*') with wider peer group and familiar adults	Identifies right choices	Indicates a want to hug with familiar others – when appropriate
H	Makes statements eliciting others' preferred options (e.g. '*What would you like?*')	Identifies wrong choices	Understands greetings of unfamiliar others

Suggested activities or strategies

Social communication

- Model simple requests by adults and peers. Use small group work or circle time to reinforce and practise. Set up situations with peers and pre-teach the child the verbal responses. For example, *'We are going to practise how to ask for help hanging your bag on your peg. Let's pretend that you have just arrived at school and cannot get to your peg. Here is Sam, he has already done his bag but is standing in your way. Let's go down to the pegs and see what this would be like. Remember there will only be three of us and in the mornings there would be many more children in the space'*. Be explicit with the child and give them choices. For example, *'Would pushing Sam out of the way be a good choice? No, a good choice would be to use your words. These are the words you could use, let's practise and see what happens'*.
- Encourage communication by the child to request help. If no communication is initiated try asking, *'Would you like some help?'* in order to encourage the early development of independent skills.

Making requests and offering suggestions

- Model asking support questions of peers. For example, in a game using construction toys ask, *'Would you like the blue one?'* Set up situations with one peer to practise this, then gradually extend the size of the group and observe from the periphery, interjecting and making a teaching point where necessary.
- Create opportunities in free play for the child to lead and be led. Guide turn-taking and invent simple Follow the Leader games in the playground, in which the AS child has an opportunity to take on the differing roles.
- Choose a familiar peer or allow the child to select a chosen friend to play alongside and practise these activities. Once the child is familiar with the skill introduce a third child to the group and allow the original two children to model the activity to the new member of the group.

Right and wrong choices

- On occasion the wrong choice may be made, such as a toy being grabbed or snatched, or an object thrown. The AS child should be taught that this is the wrong choice and given examples of the right choice to be made in this situation. Use the words, *'Do not snatch the toy, this is the wrong choice'*.
- Identify opportunities when peers are demonstrating inappropriate attention-seeking and reactions – verbalise to the child that the other pupil is making the wrong choice. Talk about what would be the right choice.
- Set up activities using photographs or small world play to teach appropriate right/wrong choices. Describe the situation. *'What are the choices the character has? Which are the right choices? Which are the wrong choices?'* Generalise the skill; ask the child to think about if they were in the situation. What would be the right and wrong choices then?
- Model situations and allow the child to identify which character is making the right/wrong choice.
- Circle time provides a good opportunity to extend this learning to a wider group.

Welcoming classroom visitors

Verbal and visual prompts are helpful to support the child. For example, prepare the child for a visitor to the classroom who is unfamiliar to them with a photograph (if possible). The visitor should be prepared with a specific format for greeting the child or group. Verbal and visual prompts will help the child understand how to identify the greeting and how to respond. This can be rehearsed in circle time and revisited. A wave or sign may need to be practised to accompany the response. Social Stories™ may also be appropriate to support the child.

Letter	What can I say? To whom and when?	Peer pressure	Growing up
I	Can use compliments to comment on appearance	Knows right and wrong choices	Changes for PE appropriately with verbal or visual prompting
I		Identifies right and wrong choices made by others	Can demonstrate modesty (e.g. knows which clothing to remove)
J	Can use compliments to comment on success	Can say firmly, 'No I don't want to'	Can demonstrate social kissing and to whom appropriate
J	Knows what not to comment on	Can accompany 'no' with appropriate body language and facial expression	Can demonstrate formal/informal social language and knows to whom each is appropriate
K	Knows how to give encouraging feedback with unknown adults in a familiar setting	Makes decision not to follow suggestions of peers if they are deemed to be the wrong choice	Can talk about physical changes in own body which may have occurred or be about to occur
K	Knows when it is not appropriate to make encouraging comments (e.g. it is not appropriate to say 'Your uniform is nice' to a police officer)	Identifies appropriate adult for support	Can talk about physical changes in bodies of opposite sex at varying stages of development
L	Is able to make requests of unfamiliar people in authority (e.g. ask a policeman for directions)	Understands the boundaries for use of inappropriate language	Understands simple emotional/hormonal changes in own body which may be about to occur
L	Is able to approach unfamiliar others for information (e.g. asking the time)	Adheres to boundaries for inappropriate language	Understands simple emotional/hormonal changes in bodies of opposite sex and approximately when they occur

Suggested activities or strategies

Modesty

- Provide a visual in the form of a flow chart for modest and discreet dressing/undressing. Use photographs or symbols of clothes and attach the visual where the child is expected to change.
- Initially, prompt the child yourself, gradually indicating the visual prompt and eventually moving away, allowing the child to use the visual prompt independently.
- It may then be appropriate to attach a small key-ring visual prompt to the PE bag as a reminder. This is also useful as a checklist for packing PE kit in the bag to take home.
- Use Social Stories™ regarding modesty to teach accepted social conventions. As the child becomes older, the degree of modesty changes, in particular for girls. Discussions and Social Stories aid the learning of this discretion.

Social language

- Model compliments and acknowledge them in peers. Relate this to the child's own feelings and those of peers.
- During team games or competitive activities, indicate peers who encourage appropriately and model the language used in these situations.
- Should inappropriate comments be made, indicate that this is inappropriate and give alternatives.

It may be useful to use a visual here of think ⟳ or speak ⟳ and indicate that it is OK to think some comments but not to say them out loud.

- Social skills groups could include activities directly related to the issue of what should and should not be spoken aloud. For example, in a shop would it be appropriate to comment out loud on the size of a lady in the queue? *'That lady in the queue is really fat.'* Would this be a thought bubble comment or a speech bubble comment? Sorting activities under the think/ say heading is useful.

Social kissing and hugging

- If the child is inappropriately kissing peers and adults, a Social Story™ is useful to indicate who it is appropriate to kiss. It is important to be very clear about who and when is appropriate, otherwise the child may think they cannot kiss anyone, including Grandma! It may be necessary to add a list of names, rather than simply indicate 'family and close friends', as this could be too general.
- Kissing and hugging among peers varies according to the age of the child. It is important that activities are built into social skills groups regarding how to read facial expressions and body language and whether these are encouraging or discouraging physical contact.
- Set up activities in which the child needs to read the body language. For example, if the peer holds their hands out wide at each side of their body, this indicates that hugging is being encouraged. Turning away indicates it is not.

Letter	What can I say? To whom and when?	Peer pressure	Growing up
M	Can use appropriate language to address unfamiliar people and request help	Understands consequences of wrong choices for self and can talk about making choices	Touching: understands areas of body on others which are appropriate to touch in social situations
M		Understands consequences of wrong choices for others and can talk about them	Touching: understands areas of own body inappropriate to touch in social situations
N	Knows it is inappropriate to ask unfamiliar people about private or personal information	Can identify risk-taking (e.g. looking at photographs and indicating where to cross the road safely)	Understands areas of others' bodies that are appropriate to touch
N		Can talk about risk and how to make a good choice	Understands areas of others' bodies that are inappropriate to touch

Suggested activities or strategies

Talking to unfamiliar others

- Set up opportunities to practise how to look at the unfamiliar adult, that is, towards the face.
- Set up opportunities for practising typical questions and formalities, such as, *'Excuse me, what is the time?'*, *'Excuse me, is this the bus to town?'*, *'Excuse me, could you tell me where the library is?'* Use role-play scenarios to create other opportunities.
- Build into this programme the possibility of change, for example, *'The last chocolate muffin has been sold, what should I do?'* If possible it is best to teach these skills in a real-life situation and it is important that parents are aware of the programme and can practise in the real world.

Identifying risk

- Use comic strip conversations either to identify situations of risk or revisit situations and identify risk. It is important in these situations that discussions involve right and wrong choices.
- Create a visual stating the options in terms of choice. The child can be involved in creating this in the form of a table or flow chart. Draw the right choice and annotate with a happy face or tick; indicate that this leads directly to a reward, and we desire these. Draw the wrong choice and annotate this with a sad face or a cross. Indicate that this leads directly to a consequence, which is something that the child doesn't like, and we don't desire or enjoy these but they have to be completed. It is important to link the right choice to rewards and the wrong choice to consequences.
- A graph is also a useful pictorial representation. Use a line graph to indicate the good and bad choices, highs and lows. Take photos each day to revisit them using the computer and give an overview of a week, month or term. Ensure the child completes the graphs themselves, while discussing what happened; they can be on paper or the whiteboard.

- Use television programmes, video, photographs and role-play scenarios to identify social situations, for example at the park, in the shop, walking to school. Identify potential risks and appropriate choices.
- Introduce the role of an appropriate peer mentor or buddying system. This can help to develop the child's independence and prevent over-reliance on adults.

Puberty

- Visuals and Social Stories™ will aid understanding of touching others. Diagrams may help understanding of the areas of the body where touching is inappropriate. It may be useful to annotate diagrams of bodies with colours, such as red for inappropriate, green for appropriate; or use ✓ and ✗ systems to identify areas of the body.
- It is important that the child knows who are 'safe' adults with whom to discuss their concerns about, and understanding of, puberty. It may be necessary to set firm boundaries around discretion.
- Explain that the onset of puberty is a difficult time, because coupled with their Autistic Spectrum characteristics they now have to come to terms with emotional changes in areas they may have already learned to understand. In particular, surges of anger may occur linked to hormone levels. Whereas once the child was able to manage this escalating feeling, or identify the triggers, now it may become much more unpredictable.
- Use visuals of changing body shapes and offer calm explanations. The child may be anxious or fearful of future changes. It is important to be truthful at this stage; to say, for example, *'I don't know exactly when these changes will happen to you, but I do know that you are going to be a man/woman'*.

Letters	Following rules	Positive and negative attention	Physical communication	Making noises
A	Sits on carpet with adult support for 3 to 5 minutes	Shows that they like verbal praise	Will hold hand and be led	Makes a quiet noise instead of crying
A	Sits on carpet independently for 3 to 5 minutes	Seeks verbal praise	Will hold hand and lead	Makes a quiet noise instead of squealing
B	Sits and listens to adults for 3 to 5 minutes	Recognises rewards	Follows pointing and direction with gaze	Makes a quiet noise instead of screaming
B	Sits and listens to peers for 3 to 5 minutes	Seeks rewards	Points to a desired object	Makes a quiet noise instead of shouting
C	Walks around school with verbal/visual prompts and reminders	Recognises negative response	Touches clothing of adult	Taps object on table while vocalising
C	Walks around school independently with occasional verbal/visual prompts	Links behaviour to negative response	Touches clothing of peer	Taps several objects while vocalising
D	Keeps hands and feet to self with visual/verbal prompts	Responds to verbal/ visual prompting and pauses negative behaviours	Taps arm of adult to gain attention	Giggles to show pleasure
D	Keeps hands and feet to self independently	Limits negative behaviour to achieve positive attention	Taps arm of peer to gain attention	Laughs to show pleasure

Suggested activities or strategies

Reinforcing rules

- Use simple, direct language to recognise good choices, using phrases such as, '*Good walking*'. Follow the child closely, saying '*Good sitting, good waiting, good writing*'; this reinforces that the action is the one required and is being rewarded by the verbal prompt. Simply saying '*Good boy*' or '*Good girl*' does not identify what the child is doing that is the correct choice.

- Allow take-up time. Sometimes you may think the child is not listening or responding to the adult request, but the child may be processing the language used. Often the AS child has a slow processing time and will need to think carefully about what has been asked of them before they can act on it.

- Repeat instructions/directions in exactly the same words – no paraphrasing. If the word order is changed or new vocabulary is used the child may have to process a new sentence or set of instructions. The child may think that a further set of instructions has been issued.

- Use a time out chair/spot/mat for inappropriate behaviours, with a timer. If an inappropriate behaviour is demonstrated (for example hitting, kicking, biting, screaming) allocate a place to be used immediately for time out. The child goes to, or is placed on, the chair/spot with a timer. No further stimulus is added. The adult does not talk to or look at the child. It may be helpful to use a visual to indicate the wrong behaviour and initially indicate this. Say '*No biting*', pointing to the visual. The time out is then not further stimulated by talk or contact; it is a time for the child to contemplate the choice they have made. Following this a discussion may be had around wrong and right choices, rewards and consequences, and the reparation activity should follow.

- Give exaggerated positive attention for the right choice of behaviours.

Using a system of rewards

- Build in rewards for maintaining focus for the duration of a timer. This can be a 'good box' with items in that the child likes, such as photographs, books, small toys, models and so on. Ensure the rewards can be met in the busy demands of a mainstream classroom. For example, it would be appropriate to have 10 minutes on the timer to look at their own choice of magazines as a reward, because this is manageable and not demanding on adult time. Riding in the playground on a scooter, on the other hand, would require adult support and could be seen as being unfair to the other children.

- Build in opportunities for the child to earn rewards and praise. Gradually move the reward more in line with the whole-school policy for rewarding children.

- Introduce 'Now, Next' cards with visual prompts. For example, 'Now *you have to sit on the carpet*. Next *you can choose from your reward box*'.

Oral and physical communication

Acknowledge all attempts to communicate (including arm-tapping, pointing and so on) and teach that it is appropriate to use your own words. Model examples. For example, '*Tapping me on the arm gets my attention, but I'm not sure I understand what you want. If you use your words to explain to me that you need to go to the toilet, I will be able to understand that much more easily.*'

- Identify appropriate classroom sounds and noises using recorded sounds and video.

- In small groups, model and rehearse appropriate sounds.

- Apply and keep firm barriers to restrict unwanted oral sounds. Use time out and a firm voice: '*No screaming*'.

- When the child is calm, model appropriate ways of gaining adult/peer attention.

- Use Social Stories™ to clarify expectations.

Letters	Following rules	Positive and negative attention	Physical communication	Making noises
E	Puts equipment away with support	Recognises positive attention in others	Knows not to pinch/nip skin of adult	Knows which noises are irritating (e.g. frequent sniffing)
E	Puts equipment away independently	Recognises negative attention in others	Knows not to pinch/nip skin of peer	Knows which noises are irritating (e.g. frequent coughing)
F	Raises hand to contribute	Can interrupt by saying 'Excuse me'	Knows not to take objects from others	Opens and closes books appropriately
F	Raises hand and waits briefly to contribute	Can interrupt by saying 'Excuse me' and waits for response	May give objects to others	Puts items down on table gently
G	Sits at table and chair to complete activity for 5 minutes	Can recognise that others look in their direction when they are listening to them	Knows not to run into a room	Knows that deliberately dropping items is irritating
G	Sits at table and chair and completes activity in a specified time	Can recognise that, as the listener, you look in the direction of the person talking	Knows not to run from room	
H	Sits appropriately in assembly for 10 minutes	Can recognise that if someone turns away, this can be a negative response	Knows not to climb onto adult	Knows that kicking chair leg is irritating
H	Takes part in assembly appropriately for 10 minutes	Understands negative body language in others	Moves face of adult towards self	Knows which behaviours are irritating

Suggested activities or strategies

Inappropriate physical contact

Inappropriate physical contact may take various forms, including pinching, nipping or biting.

- Use a time out chair/spot/mat for inappropriate behaviours, with a visual to identify the wrong behaviour if appropriate, and state firmly, '*No biting*'.
- The timer is set and no further interaction occurs. Following this, the reparation activity begins.
- Exaggerate positive attention and give rewards for the right choice behaviours.

Following rules

- Use statements of reality to reinforce the need to adhere to classroom rules, such as raising a hand before speaking. '*Look, Lucy has put her hand up; it means she wants to tell Mrs Brown something*'. Identify times when it is appropriate to raise your hand and when it is not. At circle time suggest examples such as, '*If you were sitting at the table at home, would you put up your hand to ask your mum for a drink? On the carpet in the classroom would you put up your hand to ask a question?*'
- Once a rule is understood and repeatedly demonstrated, it is useful to use a visual indicating the rule, and gradually build up the expectation of compliance.
- It is also important to build in times when a contribution is not asked for despite the hand being raised, and explicitly teach the right choice response to this.
- Gradually build up the time the child is required to sit at the table by setting up two trays, baskets or boxes. The first box contains an activity that is adult-directed, and then the second box contains the reward. Reiterate this with the language '*now/next*' and '*later*', '*work*' and '*reward*'.
- Identify the child's place in assembly and build up the time the child is required to stay there; use a visual timer. Reward the child once this has been achieved. Gradually move the adult further away until the child is able to sit independently in assembly.

Positive and negative attention

- Model examples of interrupting appropriately (for example, saying '*Excuse me ...*'). Practise with a familiar peer then a wider group in circle/carpet time.
- Model examples of listening, and give opportunities for the child to identify listening behaviour in others, for example, '*Look, Joe is showing he is listening by turning his face to the teacher*'.

Sustained inappropriate behaviours

- For sustained inappropriate behaviours, use a raised hand signal and a firmly spoken, '*Stop*'. Following this, teach what would be the right choice.
- It may also be necessary to practise the right choice with the teacher's supervision and reiterate verbally what would be the right choice. For example, if the child is running from the room, bring the child back, reiterate the right choice, model the right choice and verbalise, '*Good walking, right choice*'. Provide individualised right and wrong choice visuals. For example, when the right choice is sitting quietly, a sign could be placed on the floor in front of the child with a picture of a face with a cross over the mouth.

Letters	Following rules	Positive and negative attention	Physical communication	Making noises
I	Follows some rules for outdoor play with verbal reminders	Can identify that some parts of general group praise are relevant to them	Knows not to throw objects across room	Can join in with singing
I	Follows some rules for outdoor play independently	Reminds others when generalised praise is given	Knows not to throw object towards adult or peer	Can try to join in with whistling
J	Accepts rules about not hurting others physically and can talk about them		Knows not to push books and other items onto floor	Knows not to shout repetitively
J	Accepts rules about not hurting others verbally and can talk about them	Identifies inappropriate volume in other's voices when seeking attention		Knows not to shout randomly
K	Respects school property and can talk about rules regarding it	Is willing to revisit and talk about a situation where there may have been negative behaviours	Knows not to make others laugh by silly behaviour in the classroom	Knows not to distract others
K	Respects property of peers	Joins in with laughter at a joke		
L	Accepts that rules of playground games can change	Controls voice volume when seeking attention	Knows not to push peers	
L	Understands why rules exist for games (sport)	Laughs at a joke and knows when to stop		

Suggested activities or strategies

Following rules

The aim is that the child should learn to follow the rules independently.

- Move the child on from verbal prompts for outside play, but reiterate rules verbally. For example, '*Remember to keep your hands and feet to yourself at playtime*'. Initially it will be necessary to monitor this closely, intervening before the wrong choice is made, and verbally reminding the child of the rules.
- Make a visual display of expected rules and ensure it can be seen outside.

Discussing inappropriate behaviours

It is important to address the behaviour and teach the appropriate behaviour. Comic strip conversations are useful visuals to revisit and teach scenarios. They allow the child thinking space and help them to develop an understanding of the viewpoint of others. Comic strip conversations are helpful when revisiting situations that have gone wrong, and can identify teaching and learning points to be revisited when the child is calm and ready to access the learning.

- Colour coding in comic strip conversations is helpful in identifying the point at which a wrong choice is made, and starting a discussion around the options for other choices. It is helpful to use the colour red to identify when the child became angry (and other colours for other emotions and their increasing agitation) so that the adult can teach at which point a strategy should be used. This strategy may be talking to an adult, going to the cool-down zone, walking away, and so on, but if the child is taught when to engage this strategy when revisiting situations they will learn to manage their own emotions.

- In social skills groups set up situations and discuss choice-making opportunities. This may be in the form of role-play or visually.
- Use time out; it may be necessary for the adult to remove the child from the room and allow calm-down time before discussing what went wrong.

Voice – volume control

- Use a number scale to identify the volume of the voice in appropriate situations, from (for example) 1 = whisper in the reading corner, up to 10 = shouting at a football match. Allow the child to annotate the scale and make suggestions for different volumes.
- It may be necessary to introduce a visual volume control which has a sliding scale. This can be used to remind the child that the voice volume being used is inappropriate and needs to be adjusted or 'turned down'.
- Use verbal reminders. '*You are shouting, please use a talking voice number 5 as I find this too loud.*' '*You are whispering, please use a talking voice number 5 as I cannot hear you.*'

Letters	Following rules	Positive and negative attention	Physical communication	Making noises
M	Understands that some rules ensure safety	Recognises warnings for negative behaviours	Knows not to slap peer on back	Knows that it is inappropriate to make noises using pencil case, calculator and so on
M	Understands there will be consequences if they do not adhere to rules	Accepts warnings for negative behaviours and stops them	Knows when it is appropriate to hug peers	
N	Accepts consequences of not obeying rules	Takes responsibility for own positive behaviour and welcomes rewards	Knows not to lean on peer heavily	Accepts consequences for swearing at peers
N	Generalises rules (e.g. lining up in different places in the school, but in the same order)	Takes responsibility for own negative behaviour and accepts consequences	Knows not to lean on adult heavily	Accepts consequences for swearing at adults

Suggested activities or strategies

Using rating scales/feelings thermometers

Use rating scales to help children to take responsibility for their own behaviour, so that they can learn to control – or stop – negative behaviours appropriately. Rating scales are visual tools, which have many uses. At their simplest they show a scale from 1 to 5 with a sad face at 1 and a happy face at 5. However, they can be used to show anxiety (1 = not anxious, 5 = very anxious) or anger, calmness, frustration and virtually every other emotion.

- Create rating scales in any visual form the child enjoys.
- Discuss what the middle point (using number 3) represents, for example, *'When I talk at this number it sounds like this'* or *'When you are feeling calm at school it feels like you do now'*.
- Reflect back to the child what you think they are feeling. *'That sounds like a number 8 voice to me. Can you talk at number 5?'* or *'I think you are feeling angry, at about number 7. Do you need to go to a quiet place?'*
- Ask the child to tell you how they feel on the scale. Make sure they know which numbers should trigger actions.

Safety

- Visuals are useful to teach awareness of safety, for example, you can use photographs of the route home identifying safe places to cross the road.
- Use visuals (including video) of classrooms where practical activities are going on, identifying unsafe practices and the danger to peers.
- In the playground, identify the rules of play and the underlying dangers; consider what would be safe for the child and others. Also, teach about deliberate unsafe acts which will incur consequences to the individual.

Rules in sport

- Reiterate the rules prior to the sport and identify the person who upholds the rules. It is important to teach that this person should not be challenged and what reaction would be the right choice.
- Teach the generalisation of rules. In other words, despite a change of sport and specific associated rules, the right choice should always be made.
- It is also important to teach and discuss flexibility in some rules in differing social situations. For example, the football match of two village teams with a referee, and playground football without a referee, adhere to different rules, even though they are both football matches.

Swearing

- Teach that this language is inappropriate in school, and that the child and peers who swear have made the wrong choice and that there will be consequences. This may be a verbal reprimand, time out or more serious action depending on the nature of the incident and the school's behaviour policy.
- Set firm boundaries. Ensure that the child is aware of these and also that they are consistently adhered to by all adults.
- Discuss more appropriate language that could be used and provide lists of accepted words.
- It may be necessary to categorise the language for the child in the first instance. Do not be shocked, but treat this as a sorting activity in order that the child is certain which words are wrong choices.
- Explore jokes in social skills groups and establish those which are appropriate for school and those which are not. Clarify that swearing, even in jokes, is inappropriate in school.

Letters	Change within the classroom	Change across the day	Moving to a new class/ school	Dealing with the unexpected
A	Hangs up coat and enters classroom with support	Enters classroom quietly after conversation with adult	Identifies school from a photograph	Can enter the classroom with an adult or parent
A	Hangs up coat and enters classroom quietly and appropriately	Leaves classroom with support at end of day	Understands school is different from home	Enters classroom quietly after conversation with a TA or teacher
B	Sits on carpet or at table in classroom	Enters classroom independently	Sorts photographs of home and school	
B		Leaves classroom independently	Understands time will be spent at school without parents	Complies with requests after time out in a calm space
C	With preparation and adult support, plays in a role-play area even if the theme has been changed	Leaves classroom for playtime with support	Sort photographs of parents and teachers	
C	With verbal preparation, plays in a themed area if the theme has been changed	Can move between activities using Now and Next boards/baskets, trays or visual prompts	Associates familiar adults with school	Complies with requests within 'X' minutes without verbal resistance
D	With support, recognises own belongings even if they are not where expected	Leaves classroom for playtime independently	Identifies familiar school adults in photographs and may be able to name them	Complies and participates partially
D	Recognises own belongings even if they are not where expected	Returns to classroom after playtime independently	Associates familiar peers with school	Complies and participates fully

Suggested activities or strategies

Managing routines

- Use visual resources such as photographs of the door of the classroom, coat, coat peg or classroom. In preparation for entering the classroom, try activities to order the photographs:
  - An adult models the sequencing activity.
  - The child completes the activity with adult promptings. Try not to do the activity for the child. Although this is quicker and more efficient during the busy routines of the school day, all the child will learn from this is that, if they wait, the activity will be completed for them. Far better to invest time in teaching the child independent strategies which can be built on as they progress through the school.
- It is a good idea to move things in the classroom occasionally and prepare the child for the change. This will begin to prepare them for the understanding that objects are not always in the same place.

Managing change between activities

Use a timer to prepare the child for a change of activity, coupled with a verbal warning. For example, 'When the timer runs out playtime will end. Then we will go back to the classroom'.

- Allow take-up time for the change. Give the child an opportunity to see the change and watch peers taking part.
- Use the timer to allow time out on the appropriate chair, mat or cushion if the child can't cope with the change.
- Respond to the wrong choice with a clearly spoken 'No', using a visual if necessary. State, 'No hurting, pushing or biting'.

- Once the child is calm, calmly reiterate the right choice. For example, the child may need to enter the hall where an adult unknown to the child is taking assembly. Use the timer and allow the child to enter for a brief time (30 seconds – 1 minute), either by standing in the doorway or at the back, supported by the adult. When the time has elapsed remove the child and reward them. This process can be used to gradually build the child's confidence and compliance.

IMPORTANT NOTE: It is recommended that staff have training in order that they can safely handle or move a child should this be necessary. Different authorities use different training providers; senior managers will be aware of these and should organise training for all staff.

Unexpected visitors or changes

Allow the child to view the individual or change from a safe distance and explain why the change has happened. Reassure the child that this will not affect them and that they will be able to continue to work as usual in the classroom. In some circumstances it is simply not possible to prepare the child in advance, and this is a good lesson, as we cannot make the world totally predictable. It is important that we teach the child that they can cope in these situations, and ultimately they will learn independent strategies.

Letters	Change within the classroom	Change across the day	Moving to a new class/ school	Dealing with the unexpected
E	Leaves classroom to use toilet and returns appropriately	Leaves classroom for lunch with support	Talks about familiar peers at school	Listens to adult explanation for change
E	Uses different toilets in school if necessary	Leaves lunch room and goes to classroom with support	Understands need to go to a new school	Asks questions about changes
F	Works willingly with different adults if directed to	Leaves classroom for lunch independently	Can identify new school in a photograph and talk about it	Initiates talk about changes that have already happened
F	Works willingly with different adults	Leaves lunch room and goes to classroom independently	Understands need to move to a new classroom	Initiates talk about changes that may happen
G	Works willingly and approaches different adults for support if directed to	Works in a small group outside classroom if expected and prepared	Can talk about moving to a new class	Can talk about changes calmly and with reduced anxiety
G	Works willingly and approaches different adults for support independently	Works in a small group outside classroom if unexpected but prepared	Identifies own space in a new classroom	Talks to peers about changes
H	Works/plays with other peers if friend is absent, if directed to	Changes clothes for PE with preparation and verbal and visual support	Can talk about the new room and how it is physically arranged	Can talk and listen to peers about changes
H	Works/plays with other peers independently if friend is absent	Changes clothes for PE independently using visual prompts if necessary	Identifies new classroom from photo and talks about it	Understands that everything is not always certain

Suggested activities or strategies

Moving to a new school or classroom

- Use a planner, calendar or visual timetable to prepare for when the change will occur.
- Create photopacks and Social Stories™ for changes of new school, classrooms and important places such as toilets, the child's peg, drawer and so on. It is helpful to familiarise the child by going through these each day. Regular and frequent visits to the new environment, gradually building up the time spent there, is helpful. The child should go initially with an adult, then with the involvement of a familiar peer; gradually add more peers to make a small group.
- Be open and honest when speaking to the child and do not promise that things will always be the same. It is useful to use the term 'may'. For example, '*When we go into that classroom it may be that they will have some interesting books*'.
- Create a 'Pupil Passport' to identify strengths and weaknesses, likes and dislikes and successful strategies for support. With older pupils this encourages independence and gives a voice. Pupil passports enable the pupil to share information with any new adults.

Change across the day

- Use circle time activities to introduce the word 'may' in order to begin to understand uncertainty. Prepare and practise for any changes using discussion and giving details where possible. Show photographs and allow opportunities for raising any issues and asking questions. Be positive, refer to previous situations where the child has managed a change, and talk about how well they coped and how much they enjoyed the situation.

- Set up situations in which a change occurs, in order to teach the child coping strategies and help them begin to understand uncertainty. Don't take change away and allow the child to think they cannot cope with it, but gradually introduce changes with support. Reduce the level of support gradually, thereby increasing the child's independent strategies.
- Create flow charts of photographs or symbols to support familiar activities such as changing for PE, in order to develop independence from prompting. Attach the flow chart to the child's PE bag. The use of visual prompts is important in the long term in order that the child can develop independent strategies to move on and does not become over-reliant on adult prompting.

Prepare for disappointment

- Prepare the child for the possibility that a friend, teacher or TA may be away from school. Use Social Stories™ to explore what could happen.
- Ask parents to create opportunities out of school to experience disappointment, such as going to choose trousers or shoes, but finding that they may not be the right size. This means that the child learns to cope in everyday situations, such as when their favourite cereal or magazine is sold out at the supermarket, and can discuss alternatives (such as trying an alternative, going to a different shop or waiting until another day). It is important that parents and adults in school communicate regularly in order that work can be followed up in school and at home.

Letters	Change within the classroom	Change across the day	Moving to a new class/ school	Dealing with the unexpected
I	Remains calm during preparation discussions about daily changes	Manages changes to whole days, with preparation and support, without anxiety overload (e.g. sports day)	Finds route to new room independently	Talks about uncertainty
I	Manages changes to daily pattern of events (e.g. a teacher absent)	Manages changes to whole days independently if pre-warned (e.g. sports day)	Identifies new TA/ teacher with new classroom	Uses the word 'may' – 'it may happen' (e.g. it is an estimated journey time, we may arrive about 6 pm)
J	Copes with change to weekly pattern of events	Identifies strength of anxiety and uses a 'sensory break' or takes a timed 'break' if necessary	Identifies new adults from photographs and names them	Predicts situations where uncertainty may occur (e.g. travel times may vary depending on traffic)
J	Accepts reasons for change	Copes with change in order of subjects/lessons	Identifies peers who will be in new class/school	Prepares self with strategies for situations where uncertainty may occur (e.g. can plan to take three activities for journey, judging two may not be enough)
K	Understands and accepts why changes happen and talks about useful strategies for self-managing	Copes with changes of timings		
K	Talks and shares strategies with peers, listening to their suggestions	Understands there are inappropriate behaviours associated with change	Understands routines will change in new class/ school	Applies some strategies and talks through alternatives with adults
L	Uses personal strategies for preparing for and managing changes	Uses strategies to manage anxiety and talks about them with adults	Talks about new routine with peers and adults	Applies some strategies and talks through alternatives with peers
L	Talks about the effect of change on others	Uses strategies to manage anxiety and talks about them with peers	Discusses possible concerns/anxieties with peers and adults	Talks through a range of strategies and selects appropriate one to apply and shares suggestions

Suggested activities or strategies

Preparing for change

- Create a 'change' sticker, label or blank square for the visual timetable. This means the child can be prepared for daily changes in the routine and be proactive in writing or drawing the change which will take place.
- Use Social Stories™ in preparation for 'special' school days, such as sports day, the Christmas play and visits out. Use photographs of previous days or look at the website of the places to be visited. Bus journeys may also need careful planning in the same way. Allocating a specific seat and using a timer during the journey can be helpful.
- Use role-play in social skills groups to 'walk through' anticipated events – always using the words '*may*', '*might*', '*could*' and so on to express uncertainty.

Managing anxiety

- Teach calming strategies for dealing independently with change. For example, deep breathing techniques, Social Stories™, rating scales, modelling by adults and observations of peers.
- Practise the strategies and discuss their effectiveness. They might include: counting, visualisation exercises, breathing exercises, or taking part in a special interest activity such as looking at a favourite book or listening to music.
- Ensure the child has access to a calm area when anxiety is likely to be high.
- Teach the word and feeling 'disappointment' in social skills groups. Use visuals or photographs to discuss feelings and strategies. Strategies may include: separating the feeling from the behaviour; reiterating choices and appropriate behaviours; making suggestions for alternative activities to overcome the disappointment; talking it through.

- Allow the child to be involved in the planning process of a 'special visit' day, identifying situations where there may be uncertainty. For example, the journey time may be affected by road traffic, road closures, weather and so on. The child comes to understand that this can only be an estimated time.
- Comic strip conversations are useful in preparing situations and as a technique for teaching awareness of uncertainty in social skills groups. The cartoon scenario can be started by the adult, then the pupils complete it. Then the group share their ideas, discussing where appropriate choices should be made.
- Hold discussion or role-play groups exploring scenarios based on coping in anxious situations, and discuss when to use appropriate strategies.

Moving school

- Allow the child to take part in the preparation of and modelling of their own Social Stories™, sharing these with peers or younger children.
- When the child visits a new school and meets new staff, give them the opportunity to create their own photograph pack. Allow the child to take responsibility for the camera and taking the photographs. This gives the child ownership of the task. They may also identify objects and places that are of importance to them, which may not necessarily be of a similar importance to the adult. For example, for security the child may like to take a photograph of where to go if they feel unwell. Some children like to take a photograph of the fire extinguisher; this alleviates any anxieties they have. These would not necessarily be on the adult's agenda for the photo pack.

Letters	Change within the classroom	Change across the day	Moving to a new class/ school	Dealing with the unexpected
M	Suggests strategies for others if prepared for change	Explains strategies for others if prepared for change	Attends visits with support and asks questions	Understands strategies for coping with change which may happen
M			Attends visits independently and asks questions	
N	Understands and copes with unexpected change	Understands and copes with unexpected change	Attends new intake days with support of new staff	Has a range of strategies for personal coping skills
N	Suggests strategies for others to help understand and cope with unexpected change	Suggests strategies for others to help understand and cope with unexpected change	Attends new intake days and uses strategies for independent coping skills	Suggests a range of strategies for coping skills to others

Suggested activities or strategies

Planning for change

- Allow the pupil to be proactive in preparation for changes. They may take their own photos, and prepare questions prior to and after the visit. In preparation for the visit the child may like to keep a note of any questions they think of and put them in a notebook or on a laptop or tablet computer. On the day of the visit the child may like to take the questions with them. They may like to tick off the questions as they are met in general discussion, and raise any others when appropriate if they have not been answered.
- Teach the pupil to use a diary or a planner to show organisation and plan ahead. This may need to be modelled and explained on several occasions and checked at first. Some AS children like the structure that this gives them, and are very efficient at using diaries. Others find the organisational aspect difficult to manage and need much more prompting and guidance before this strategy becomes useful to them.
- Continue to give opportunities for discussion in social groups with peers. This is essential; it provides a safety net for the child to try out any ideas and strategies and gives the adult an opportunity to observe and make assessments and judgements about how the child is managing. It gives the child an opportunity to share what they have learned with peers and builds self-confidence.

Managing anxiety

- Teach **Problem + talk = Problem shrinks**
- Teach that it is OK to feel anxious, cross, frustrated or disappointed, but it is not OK to shout, throw things and so on. Separate the feeling from the action. Use the strategy of a sensory break and allow the child to calm down before teaching about choices. Encourage the child to attempt a small part of the activity in order to gain a feeling of success.
- In PSHE lessons allow peers to share strategies for dealing with anxiety and identifying levels of anxiety. Discuss outcomes and associated feelings.
- Teach the child to use a number line to identify the strength of the feeling. Identify physical symptoms of the escalating feeling, for example, sweaty hands, tight head, quicker breathing, quicker pulse rate. Identify on the number line when it is appropriate to use a strategy or make a choice.

Letters	Personal hygiene	Personal space	Organising belongings	Personal responsibility
A	Indicates underwear is wet. Moves to toilet area if underwear is wet	Prefers to play away from others	Carries own belongings into classroom	Carries own belongings into classroom
A	Indicates underwear is soiled. Moves to toilet area if underwear is soiled	Plays alone in the classroom environment		
B	Goes to toilet when asked/reminded	Allows others to play close by	Hangs up own coat and book bag	Hangs up own coat and book bag
B	Asks to use toilet	Allows others to play close by and will glance towards them	Finds own coat and book bag at end of day	Finds own coat and book bag at end of day
C	Goes to toilet independently	Allows others to play side by side	Places belongings in own drawer/tray	Places belongings in own drawer/tray
C	Washes hands independently after toileting	Allows others to play side by side and may pass a toy	Collects belongings in own drawer/tray	Collects belongings in own drawer/tray
D	Accepts washing hands at other times of day	With support, allows others to share resources which are not being used	Places water bottle in correct place	Follows simple routines and instructions with verbal prompting (e.g. sitting on carpet, listening)
D	Uses toilet independently	Takes turns if prompted and guided by an adult	Returns water bottle to correct place once used	Follows simple routines and instructions with verbal and visual prompting

The Target Ladders

Suggested activities or strategies

Toilet training

- Specific reward charts are useful in the first instance for encouragement. You can place a visual reward chart in the toilet cubicle. Tokens recorded on the chart can accumulate to earn a concrete reward. If the child likes cars, use car stickers and verbal praise.
- Use photographs of the toilet for familiarity, including photographs of wet soiled knickers and the toilet where toileting has been completed successfully. The photographs are then annotated with ✓ or ✗ or ☺ or ☹, denoting the right and wrong choices. The visual and practical nature of this activity is often very helpful.
- Place visual flow charts in the toilet cubicles and over the hand basins showing the process to be followed when using the toilet and washing hands.
- Social Stories™ are also very helpful in encouraging independent toileting. There are also DVDs available. They need to be used frequently at first in order for the child to associate themselves with the skills in the story.

Sharing with peers

If the child finds it difficult to play alongside others, allow the child to become fully engrossed in a toy and then move a peer into the space. Gradually increase the time and then decrease the distance.

Developing routines

- Before expecting a child to develop a skill (for example, hanging up their coat) you should first model the activity and accompany it by a verbal explanation.
- Then indicate peers doing the desired activity. *'Look, Alice is hanging up her coat.'*
- You can use 'backwards chaining', in which an adult does all but the last stage of the task and leaves the child to be successful by completing the task. Gradually, the adult completes less and less, allowing the child to take increased responsibility for the activity.
- Then allow the child to complete the task with verbal prompts.
- Produce a visual prompt to enable the child to complete the tasks independently.
- It may be useful to have a flow chart or visual timetable of the morning routine and look at this first before completing the tasks. This is best done in a quiet place without the stimulation of the other children in the class. Then use the flow chart to prompt the child through the activities. It is good to introduce reliance on strategies at an early stage, before the child becomes dependent on adult help. This encourages independence and problem-solving for the future.
- Build in rewards for each successful step.
- Display photographs of a child completing the right choice, such as washing their hands or hanging up their coat, to reinforce the behaviour.
- Identify rewards for specific behaviour, if one is presenting a problem. Link the reward to areas of interest, for example, using the car ramp for 5 minutes with a visual timer.

Letters	Personal hygiene	Personal space	Organising belongings	Personal responsibility
E	Accepts right and wrong choices for putting things in mouth	Engages in co-operative play/work alongside another child	Uses visual prompts to collect belongings at the end of the day	Makes the right choice when offered two options
E	Can talk about brushing own teeth	Allows another to share resources that are not being used	Is less reliant on visual prompts for support	Accepts consequences of making the wrong choice
F	Can talk about how to wash body when bathing or showering	Plays/works co-operatively with another child if guided by an adult	Can identify belongings that belong to others	Complies with familiar adult's requests when calm
F	Can talk about when to wear clean clothes	Plays/works co-operatively with another independently	Can return others' belongings to them or their bags	Can talk about complying with adult requests
G	Can talk about when it is appropriate to wash body	Organises belongings on table space away from others	Carries own PE/swimming bag	Can accept responsibility for what they do, when calm
G	Can talk about when washing of body is needed	Organises belongings on a table in close proximity to others, leaving a small space between	Can unpack own belongings from swimming/PE bag	Can talk about reasons for not following all peer directions
H	Is aware of discretion when changing for PE	Shares resources that are currently being used	Can return belongings/clothing to own PE/swimming bag using visual prompt or checklist	Identifies the wrong choice and explains why it is inappropriate
H	Is able to change discreetly for PE	Shares resources in a small group and allows others to use desired item; waits turn	Can return belongings/clothing to own PE/swimming bag independently	Knows that making excuses or blaming others is inappropriate

Suggested activities or strategies

Use visuals for personal hygiene

- Find photographs and symbols of brushing hair, washing, and so on for talking about and sorting.
- Take photographs of specific problems (muddy hands, muddy legs, dirty unkempt hair) and the solutions (soap and sink, bath of water, shampoo and brush).
- Create opportunities for practising using toys, such as dog and brush, doll and brush.
- Mix up the photographs of problems and solutions and ask the questions:
  - What is wrong/the problem?
  - What does he/she need to do?
- Use small world toys for the child to demonstrate that they can follow visual sequences for personal hygiene. Encourage the child to talk through the options aloud and make suggestions that could be appropriate or inappropriate, linking this to the outcomes.

Visual prompts for organisation

- Use visual prompts, flow charts or checklists for PE/swimming. These can be threaded onto a key-ring and attached to the sports bag. They can be placed in the area of the classroom where the child changes or attached by tape to the back of the chair used to place their clothes on.

Making choices

- If the child makes a wrong choice, explain verbally that this is the wrong choice and give alternative suggestions for the right choice.
- Use photographs of scenarios to talk through the situation and the choice of options. The SEAL resources in schools have excellent photographs of children in a variety of everyday situations. These are good starting points for individual and group discussions. They will help the child to generalise the skill they are learning and put them into context in day-to-day situations. Talk about transferring the skill into a situation that may occur out of school and the choices that they could make.

- Use visuals to indicate right choice = reward, wrong choice = consequences. Discuss in groups the meanings of these words and the direct relevance to themselves. For example, do we feel happy and enjoy a consequence or is it something that is best avoided?
- In circle time and social skills groups discuss the word 'responsible' and link this to the right choice.
- Use DVD extracts from children's television programmes to talk about choices. Identify characters that make the right/wrong choice.
- Use comic strip conversations to identify wrong choice-making in situations, and the consequences and associated feelings.

Taking responsibility

- Social Stories™ are helpful to understand the issues around making excuses, blaming others and so on. They will positively reinforce and encourage the child to take responsibility for their actions.
- Create opportunities in circle time and social skills groups for discussions involving questions such as:
  - What would be the right choice?
  - What would happen?
  - What would be the wrong choice?
  - What would happen?
  - How would you feel?
  - How would they feel?
- You can also hold comic strip conversation sessions to explore these questions.
- Use circle time activities to reiterate right choices.
- Use social skills groups to explore right and wrong choices through role-play/ DVDs/puppets/photographs and pictures of scenarios.

Letters	Personal hygiene	Personal space	Organising belongings	Personal responsibility
I	Is able to recognise that peers may wish for privacy when changing	Moves away if someone comes too close		Is responsible and takes care of own belongings
I	Knows there is a range of hygiene products		Puts own belongings into bag and prepares to go home	Talks about responsible and irresponsible behaviours
J	Covers mouth when coughing or sneezing, and understands why	Keeps appropriate distance from familiar adults	Delivers and uses home/school communication book or reading journal	Talks about responsible classroom behaviours and takes part in role-plays/discussion
J	Knows how to dispose of tissues safely and does this	Keeps appropriate distance from familiar peers	Organises all own belongings in school prior to returning home (e.g. coat, bag, lunch box, water bottle, homework)	Talks about irresponsible classroom behaviours and takes part in role-plays/discussions
K	Knows about personal hygiene related to private areas of body	Understands personal space is wider with unfamiliar others	Organises belongings for each day at home with support	Makes appropriate choices and takes responsibility for own behaviours (negative or positive)
K	Is discreet when washing/showering (e.g. following swimming)		Organises belongings prior to school day independently	Is responsible if asked to be somewhere or bring something
L	Can discuss making decisions to take a bath or shower appropriately and independently	Understands the more familiar the other, the smaller the personal space becomes	Is aware that different belongings are needed on different days (e.g. PE days, swimming days, music days)	Is trustworthy and takes care of others' belongings
L	Can make decisions to wash appropriately and independently		Can organise different belongings for different days	

Suggested activities or strategies

Understanding hygiene

- Social Stories™ are helpful when teaching appropriate ways to deal with coughing and sneezing.
- Display visual flowcharts showing the safe and hygienic disposal of tissues above the bin, and near where tissues are kept in the classroom.
- Use Social Stories regarding personal hygiene.
- Talk to the parents and explain what you have taught. Ask the child to demonstrate and encourage parents to continue with some verbal and visual prompts at home in the bedroom and bathroom.

Growing up

- Visual resources used in PSHE, SED and SEAL, including DVDs, are likely to be useful when teaching about issues related to growing up.
- Be prepared to answer questions frankly and without embarrassment. The child needs to clarify what is meant and may be very literal in their understanding.
- In social skills groups, talk about discretion. Identify the appropriate adults who can be asked questions about personal matters: teachers, TAs, family members. Identify inappropriate adults, such as unknown adults. Be specific in your identifications. The bus driver may be 'known' to the child, but he is not an appropriate person to be asked these questions.

Personal space

- Set up scenarios with unfamiliar/familiar adults. Discuss problems such as these:
  - Where would you sit – how far away?
  - Could you lean on them?
  - Would it be OK to place your pudding on their lunch tray while you ate your main course?

  Use visuals where possible and include reference to feelings in the discussion. Annotate the visuals with a ✓ or ✗ denoting the right and wrong choices, or ☺ or ☹ as an indication of feelings.

- It may be necessary to give the child a reference point for personal distances. The length between your hand and elbow is the gap to leave between your bodies when you are talking to someone face to face.

Organisation

- Prompts are useful in helping children to organise themselves, and these can take the form of visuals or checklists. Sticky notes can be attached to a planner to indicate that a message or letter needs to be handed over.
- Teach the child to use a diary/calendar/timetable/checklist to prepare at home. This enables them to rely on strategies rather than adult prompting, and to organise themselves for differing days.
- As the child matures, show them how to use their mobile phones for setting reminders.

Responsibility

- Give the child a checklist and prompts to support taking care of their own belongings.
- Set up scenarios in social skills groups to indicate responsible/irresponsible behaviours. Use DVD extracts and visuals/photographs depicting clear examples. This can lead to less clear examples where the boundaries are not so precise, and discussion of points-of-view can follow.
- Role-play allows exploration of the issues, but it may be necessary to allow AS children to play themselves if they find it difficult to take an alternative role.
- Practise responsible ways to do chores/make deliveries/take messages in school. Give opportunities to practise these skills initially between familiar adults and with familiar routines. Progress this by gradually introducing new adults and less familiar surroundings and routines.

Aspect 5: Personal organisation

Letters	Personal hygiene	Personal space	Organising belongings	Personal responsibility
M	Makes decisions and understands the reasons for good personal hygiene	Allows others into personal space	Knows where to go and who to ask to retrieve lost belongings	Is trustworthy – can keep something in confidence. Can talk about some confidences that must be told to an adult for safety
M	Can talk about some germs and diseases and has some understanding of how they are spread	Discusses coping strategies for allowing others into personal space	Use appropriate strategies to search for lost belongings	Thinks things through and makes good choices and judgements
N	Understands changes needed for personal hygiene associated with puberty	Understands size of own personal space can change	Uses planner/journal to organise homework and home to school communication	Shows parents that they can be trusted
N	Knows how and where to use appropriate products associated with puberty	Can ask for own personal space if necessary	Relies on homework planner for prompting	Shows adults in school they can be trusted

Suggested activities or strategies

Approaching puberty

Photographs, flow charts and visual resources are important when teaching personal hygiene associated with puberty.

- It is important that the child has individual adult support and pre-teaching prior to any lessons relating to puberty. They may need individual adult support to discuss any misconceptions. The adult will need to be confident in this area of teaching and not feel in any way embarrassed by questions that may arise. Discussion about where and when to ask questions, and issues of discretion, may be necessary – it is not always appropriate to ask such questions. Make a list of trusted adults in school and at home who can be asked questions of this nature.
- Arrange access to a range of products used during puberty, be these deodorants, facial creams or sanitary ware. Time to explore these and ask questions is essential. In particular, girls with sensory difficulties may like to feel the products to see which ones feel best next to their skin.
- It may be necessary to make the first session brief and then allow time for take-up and thought. Follow this with more extended sessions as the child becomes more comfortable and willing to ask questions, allowing them to guide the session with their questions.

Personal space social skills groups

In social skills groups, explore the amount of 'personal space' each child needs. This tends to be around the length of the forearm in social conversation, although it is much closer when queuing. With unfamiliar people, it tends to be further.

Developing strategies for organising

- Offer explicit teaching of strategies for finding 'lost' items within the context of the school.
- Give explicit teaching of strategies for organisation, with sharing sessions between peers and adults. Explain that being organised is a useful life strategy. Use a diary/planning document and show this to the child, demonstrating how it can be used. A diary or planner is a reliable prompt in circumstances when the teacher or other school adult is not present to give reminders to the child.

Confidences

It may be useful to identify 'good' and 'bad' secrets, and identify safe adults both in and out of school.

- Social Stories™ and comic strip conversations are helpful. Set up scenarios such as this one: *'Sarah told John a secret. She knows that someone in their class has taken her friend's ruler. What should she do/say? What should John do/say? How do the individuals feel?'*
- Set up opportunities for role-play to explore the making of good choices and judgements in social situations, both in school and in the community. It may be necessary to allow AS children to play themselves, if they are not comfortable playing a role.

Letters	Emotional literacy	Anxiety	Anger/frustration	Coping with 'no'
A	Can point to a picture of a happy face in others	Watches others as they start new activity	Recognises an angry face in self, using a mirror, photograph or film	Recognises 'no' signal from familiar adult
A	Can point to a sad face in others	Attempts a change of familiar activity with adult support	Recognises an angry face in peer	Recognises 'no' spoken
B	Makes a happy face on request	Attempts unfamiliar activities with adult support	Knows what anger feels like	Uses 'no' signal to refuse an activity
B	Makes a sad face on request	Will attempt to repeat an unfamiliar activity a second time	Can identify 'things that make me angry'	Uses spoken 'no' to refuse an activity
C	Points to a character in a book who is showing a happy face	Attempts new activities with peers but shows anxiety	Knows it is OK to feel angry	Knows there is a consequence to ignoring adult's 'no'
C	Identifies a sad face in a story book	Attempts new activities with peers	Knows there are good and bad ways of showing anger	Knows there is a consequence to refusing to do something
D	Recognises a fearful/ scared face in others	Is able to recognise worried/anxious/nervous face	Can say what makes familiar adults angry	Accepts the consequence of ignoring 'no' but may comment or use facial expression
D	Recognises an angry face in others	Can talk about a worried character in a story book	Knows what makes friends angry	Accepts the consequence of saying 'no'

Suggested activities or strategies

Teaching emotional literacy

- Photographs of a variety of faces are helpful, starting with people who are happy, sad, angry, scared. These can be used to familiarise the child with facial expressions and emotional literacy.
- Play games such as Snap, matching pairs, or Kim's game, using photographs of people with the different expressions.
- Use familiar picture/story books and identify the faces in the pictures.
- Talk about how 'happy' feels and identify times when the child feels happy.
- Take photographs of the child when happy (for example on the trampoline, swimming, receiving a reward) and use this as a reference point. Associate the photograph with the feeling. Then move on to another feeling.
- Make a photograph book of the child, family members and adults in school showing feelings. When looking at the book, talk about the facial expressions and ask the question, *'How do they feel?'*

Pre-empting anxiety

- Prepare for new activities that may make the child anxious, with photographs and Social Stories™.
- Support the child when attempting a new activity, giving encouragement and praise. Spend a brief amount of time on the new activity then return to a familiar one, but revisit the new activity frequently, gradually extending the amount of time spent on it.
- Make a scale showing nervous/anxious visuals (photographs or symbols) and show how the strength of feeling is reduced as the child makes further attempts at an activity.
- Noise may cause anxiety in new situations, for example, singing/clapping in assembly, shouting/cheering in PE. Prepare the child for the noise by talking about it. Ear defenders are also helpful in dulling loud noises and reducing anxiety and fear.
- Use familiar books to identify anxiety or nervousness in characters. Teach through the story that the anxiety reduces with familiarisation.

Coping with anger

- For anger, repeat the suggestions above for anxiety, beginning with identification of facial expressions and body language using photographs.
- Teach that it is OK to feel angry. It is not OK to express that anger in certain ways such as biting, kicking, hitting, throwing things in anger. Separate the action from the feeling.
- Teach strategies for coping with and managing feelings of anger. It is your anger and you must learn to control it. Have a safe calm place to go to, if that is appropriate for the child. Involve the child in choosing or creating the space. It could be as simple as a sheet over a table, a bean bag in the book corner or a special calm chair. A Dark Den or tent can be purchased or some schools have a designated room: a 'calm room' fitted with calming lights and cushions.

Teaching 'no'

- When teaching 'no' use a calm, firm voice. It is often useful to accompany this with a hand signal (the flat of the hand raised towards the child and kept in place). You may like to use a visual sign instead of the hand that is held up. Give the child time to process the verbal instruction and recognise the visual signal; if necessary repeat the instruction exactly, accompanied by the chosen visual sign in exactly the same way.
- Teach that it is appropriate (the right choice) to respond to the adult 'no' instruction. This is the right choice and is rewarded.
- Teach that not responding appropriately (making the right choice) to 'no' is the wrong choice and there are consequences.
- In circle/carpet time set up situations to talk about why the adult said 'no', in order to introduce safety awareness.
- Encourage talking. Explain to the child it is important that they 'use their words'. This helps adults to understand what is in their head and then allows the adults to help them.
- Teach that just because an idea is in their head doesn't mean it is in the adult's head, unless the child has told them.

Letters	Emotional literacy	Anxiety	Anger/frustration	Coping with 'no'
E	Makes a frightened/ scared face	Identifies physical feelings of anxiety (e.g. hot/tight head)	Can accept adult support and direction when angry	Understands the same choice will always be met with 'no'
E	Makes an angry face		Can communicate by talking to an adult when angry	Can identify from a group of photographs 'no' activities (e.g. climbing on the wall in the playground)
F	Identifies a frightened/ scared face in a story book	Can identify progression of anxious feelings	Is able to allow peer close to them when angry	Complies with 'no' and does not persistently revisit activity
F	Identifies an angry face in a story book	Talks about progression of anxious feelings to an adult or friend	Is able to acknowledge peer following anger	Points to an activity, and says 'no' or says why it is not allowed
G	Identifies behaviours associated with happy and sad	Knows peers are anxious by their body language and face	Talks about anger and what it feels like (e.g. faster heart rate)	Understands there are right and wrong choices in response to 'no'
G	Identifies behaviours associated with scared and angry	Is able to talk to peers about their anxiety	Listens to others talk about their anger and contributes suggestions, strategies	Sorts photographs of right and wrong choices under headings (e.g. kicking a chair/ looking quietly at a book)
H	Talks about four basic feelings and explains what they feel like to them	Is able to seek/involve appropriate adult when anxious	Begins to recognise stages of own anger using a number scale	Revisits and talks about responses to 'no'
H	Talks about what makes them feel the four basic feelings	Is able to seek/involve appropriate adult when peer is anxious	Begins to recognise build-up in own anger and links this to own physical attributes using a number scale	Suggests some activities which may mean an adult will respond with 'no'

Suggested activities or strategies

Scaling emotions

- Begin to teach that emotions have a range of strengths, which can change. The feeling can increase and decrease. Use a number line, initially 1 to 3. Help the child to use this to identify the strength of the feeling. They may prefer to use words at this stage (cool, warm, hot). Gradually extend the range to include more numbers (1 to 10) or more words.
- Make an anger thermometer. Annotate this with the physical feelings and changes the child experiences, in order to begin to identify escalating feelings. For example, fingers tingle, hands feel hot, head feels tight, pulse gets quicker.
- Identify a time during the escalating feelings when it becomes too powerful for the child to engage with a strategy or talk to an adult. For example, *'When I get to 6 out of 10 I'm about to lose my temper and throw something or shout, and it is too difficult for me to talk to an adult and tell them what is wrong at this point. If I go to my calming place this helps and then I can talk about it later'*.
- Comic strip conversations are useful in identifying escalating feelings and identifying when to use a strategy to stop the escalation and begin to de-escalate.
- Comic strip conversations are also helpful in teaching right and wrong choices associated with emotional outbursts.
- Social Stories™ are helpful for teaching strategies associated with right and wrong choices.

Sensory breaks

- A sensory break system is useful in helping a child to manage their emotions.

The child manages their own sensory break based on an understanding of their escalating feelings. The child indicates with a sign, symbol or verbally that they need to take a break. The child is aware how long each break lasts for, where it can be taken and how many are allocated each day.

- When the child indicates a need for a sensory break this is not disputed by the adult. The child goes to the designated sensory break space with a timer. This time is not stimulated by talk and the adult monitors the child at a distance. When the allotted time has elapsed the child may wish to talk about the problem. The expectation is that the child then returns to the lesson and activity.
- It is helpful to have an identified time out/break or calming area at playtimes and lunchtimes and during lessons away from the classroom such as PE. This may be a different place to the one used during lesson times. You can identify a bench or place in the playground; it may be helpful to have a visual sign indicating it is a calm area for all the children. For PE, take a chair, cushion or beanbag outside, or identify a place with a hoop on the grass. This means the child is aware there is a place allocated and this prevents them wandering away.

Anger management

- Teach alternative and appropriate strategies for coping with escalated anger and calming down. These should be appropriate to the environment and school, so that they cause minimal distraction to other children and adults. They might include: pacing, popping bubble wrap, squeezing a stress ball, squeezing modelling clay. When one of these strategies is used, verbalise that this is the *'Right choice'* and reward it.
- In social skills groups, set up scenarios and role-plays to teach right choices of behaviour associated with anger.
- Use DVDs to identify angry emotions and discuss the inner feelings of the characters and the choices they are making.
- Identify adults in school who are available for support. It may be helpful at playtimes and lunchtimes to have an identified adult who is always stationed in the same area of the playground for the child to turn to if necessary. Fluorescent jackets are helpful in identifying this person from a distance.

Letters	Emotional literacy	Anxiety	Anger/frustration	Coping with 'no'
I	Identifies a wider range of feelings (e.g. excitement, anxiety)	Is able to use anxiety scale to pinpoint current strength of feeling	Recognises increasing anger in peers	Listens to explanation of why 'no'
I	Talks about physical feelings associated with wider range of emotions	Begins to control behaviour of anxiety	Recognises physical anger attitudes in others	Acknowledges and accepts explanation of why 'no'
J	Begins to realise some behaviours associated with emotions are appropriate	Can bring anxious behaviour to a halt when asked	Begins to understand anger can be also frustration	Accepts a verbal response to 'no' is inappropriate (as a response to an instruction from an adult in authority)
J	Is able to talk about right and wrong choices for behaviour associated with emotions	Can bring anxious behaviour to a halt independently using strategies such as breathing exercises	Discusses scenarios in which they may be angry/frustrated	Understands why a physical response to 'no' is inappropriate
K	Is able to act out emotions in scenarios and small groups	Takes part in creating own Social Stories™ to calm anxiety	Knows there are consequences for wrong choices	Accepts 'no' without further negotiation
K	Uses role-play to identify points at which good choices could be made	Uses talking to reduce anxiety	Knows when and how to make the right choices	Talks about accepting 'no' and reasons why this is the right choice
L	Is able to revisit personal situations involving feelings and discuss	Uses appropriate physical activity to reduce anxiety independently	Knows strategies for dealing with and reducing their own anger	Accepts 'no' without inappropriate facial response or gesture
L	Is able to revisit and identify triggers for feelings	Explores appropriate physical activity to reduce anxiety in the school environment	Uses strategies successfully to reduce anger	Talks about right and wrong choices for facial expressions or gestures in response to 'no'

Suggested activities or strategies

Strategies for controlling emotions

- Set up situations for associating the appropriate words with feelings. For example, '*When the last of the sponge pudding was taken by the boy before you in the dinner queue the feeling you felt was disappointment*'.
- Teach and practise a range of strategies for dealing with extreme emotions, such as: calm breathing, physical activity, looking through a book, using a stress ball.
- Use a feelings line with a range 1 to 10 and symbols indicating feelings. Use this visual resource to ask for feedback on DVDs and role-play situations. '*Show me on the feelings line how you think the character is feeling. What number do you think the feeling is at?*' (Numbers indicate the strength of the feeling, 10 being high.)

Good and bad choices

- The feelings line coupled with comic strip conversations are useful techniques to revisit situations. These are especially helpful for reflecting on social times as they give the adult a good insight into the incident and the perceptions of the child.

This can then be used to identify when a wrong choice may have been made and when a right choice could have been made. A discussion can then take place about what the right choices could be.

- A post box or box with a lid can be helpful if the child finds it difficult to let issues drop and keeps revisiting them. The problem is written or drawn on a piece of paper and posted into the box. The action means that the adult will take the problem away and deal with it. The adult will give the child feedback about the resolution but the child no longer needs to think or worry about the problem. Sometimes the physical act of actually shredding the paper when the issue has finally been resolved allows the child to let go.
- In social skills groups, set up role-plays to act out right and wrong choices. The child may prefer to play themselves initially in these situations if they have difficulty with other points of view.

Anxiety

Always acknowledge the child's anxiety and remain calm, be positive and refer to examples of when the child has successfully managed their anxiety, however small the steps. Allow the child to feel confident when talking through their anxiety and develop a relationship of trust. The child needs to be aware the adult will support them and will not push them too far too quickly, as this will increase anxiety.

- Support the child through the early stages of a new activity and encourage positive small steps in order to make long-term progress.
- Prepare the child carefully, choosing the timing of the preparation with care. Beginning to prepare too early may increase the child's anxiety, as they may begin to think and worry about it immediately. Keep parents well-informed and provide information for home to support the positive steps forwards. For example, if the child is worried about taking part in a swimming lesson:
  - Take the child to look at the pool and allow them to play in the space, look at a book and so on in order to become familiar with the environment.
  - Next, let the child observe the lessons from a distance, then gradually watching closer to the pool.
  - Allow them to handle the equipment and floats on dry land.
  - Allow the child to change but not to enter the water, then to dip their toes in, and thus very slowly and gradually introduce them to the water.
- Slowly extend the activities session by session, always being positive and listening to any further anxieties the child may raise. This is intensive in terms of adult time initially, but will result in long-term positive benefits for the child, and the skills can then be transferred and generalised to other situations in which anxiety may occur. '*Remember that you used to be scared of the swimming pool and how confident you are now? We can use what you have learned to help you to try tennis.*'

Letters	Emotional literacy	Anxiety	Anger/frustration	Coping with 'no'
M	Understands views of others and emotions being experienced	Knows range of strategies to reduce anxiety	Revisits personal situations and identifies triggers for anger	Accepts and understands reasoning from adults behind 'no' and can discuss with peers
M	Understands others may have different feelings inside, associated with emotion	Talks about strategies to reduce anxiety with peers	Accepts and understands 'no' from unfamiliar adult	Accepts and understands reasoning from peers behind 'no' without further explanation
N	Supports others with feelings	Recognises triggers for anxiety in advance	Discusses scenarios and identifies potential triggers	Can talk about the reasons for adults saying 'no' and what this means and how to respond
N	Adapts own feelings when supporting others	Uses a range of strategies to reduce anxiety	Accepts and understands 'no' from unfamiliar peer	

Suggested activities or strategies

Peer and adult mentoring

- Set up a peer mentoring system with pre-arranged dates to meet and an 'agenda'. The adult attends as a facilitator only. This helps to:
  - create a supportive network for the child;
  - reduce challenging behaviours;
  - enable the child to deal with a variety of social challenges;
  - increase the child's understanding of their own behaviour;
  - enable the child to make more choices;
  - encourage social interaction with peers;
  - encourage independence from adults.
- Set up an adult mentoring programme. This gives the child time to talk through any issues which may be troubling them. The session can be ended with a period of time in which to talk about their own personal or special interests. If the child talks at length, this is a good opportunity to teach the structure of social communications, allowing the listener to comment and ask questions. Sometimes it is helpful to time this conversation and set a structure at the outset with tick boxes of parts to be covered in the conversation. For example: you speak, I ask a question, you answer the question, you tell me some more, I make a comment or suggestion, the talk is ended as time has finished.
- In social skills groups, set up scenarios. Explain the situation, model an example, allow the group to be involved in role-play or discussion, then review. Reiterate the importance of choice-making and how the right choice is rewarded.

Calming strategies

Explore calming strategies in small groups. Discuss and try self-talk, music, television, a game, drawing, reading, talking to others, and thinking of pleasant images. Try out the strategies and rank them or give them a score according to their effectiveness for each individual. Allow the group to discuss their opinions and discuss any additional strategies they have found to be personally effective.

Identifying triggers

- Use books, photographs, cartoon strips or DVDs to identify triggers for anger/anxiety. Talk about strategies for avoiding the triggers, changing them and learning to deal with them.
- Set up groups to discuss dealing with frustrating work, or with losing items, and useful strategies. Encourage the child to communicate and talk about a problem with adults, to enable the adults to support the child.
- Set up groups to discuss dealing with criticism from adult and peers. Talk about the feelings involved and appropriate reactions and what to do next. Discuss making the right choices in these situations and identifying and talking to appropriate adults.

Letters	Body language	Communicating without speaking	Physical space	Intonation and word stress/expression
A	Shows recognition of waving and may join in	Nods head for 'yes'	Plays in own space with toys	Responds to a cross voice
A	Responds to hand held out to follow/join activity	Shakes head for 'no'	Plays in own space with toys but may glance towards others	Imitates a cross voice
B	Recognises and uses nod as 'yes'	Indicates 'I want' by pointing or picture communication	Allows others to play nearby with familiar/ same toys	Joins in with songs and rhymes
B	Recognises and uses shake of head as 'no'; also hand signal for 'stop'	Copes well when 'I want' is denied	Allows others to play nearby with familiar/ same toys. Glances in their direction	Can 'lower' own voice (e.g. imitate in song/ action rhymes)
C	Recognises and uses a smile for approval/ permission	Uses Now and Next board with adult support	Knows not to sit on some adults	Demonstrates understanding of intonation when singing to self
C	Recognises a frown	Chooses reward from choice of two for Now and Next board	Knows not to lean on some adults, with help	
D	Recognises arms wide as encouragement for a hug	Tries to imitate some speech/sounds	Knows not to lean on some peers, with help	Repeats speech back to adult independently
D	Reciprocates wide arms to ask for hug	Tries to imitate syllables	Knows not to lean on people without reminders	Copies intonation during echolalia (repeated speech or verbal sounds)

Suggested activities or strategies

Understanding rewards

- Set up a choice board with photographs of favourite toys and activities. Encourage the child to point to the desired toy, and the adult then says the name aloud. The child is then given the toy. Gradually encourage the child to collect the choice board (which is always found in the same place) and indicate what they want. Ask, '*What do you want [Joseph]?*' Once the child has indicated their choice, say, '*I want castle*'. Reward the child with the toy or activity.
- Set up two boxes, baskets or trays. Attach visual symbols and colour coding indicating 'Now' and 'Next'. The Next tray contains the reward, for example, a favourite toy, to motivate. The Now tray contains an activity chosen by the adult, the work.
- The Now work activity must be completed before the Next, which is the reward. In the early stages the Now activity must be very easy to complete and lots of praise and reward is used to motivate. For example, merely completing the last piece of a puzzle. This allows the child to begin to understand that complying with adult-directed tasks results in rewards. It also prepares the child well for working in the classroom on adult-directed tasks. A visual timer and a warning can be helpful when the rewards time needs to come to an end.

Sitting and leaning

If the child sits or leans on adults and peers inappropriately, indicate that this is not appropriate and give clear direction. '*You are leaning on me. I can't use my arm. Please sit up.*' '*Look, the other children are sitting on their chairs.*'

- If the child is allowed to sit on your knee or lean against you at some times, make it clear when this is allowed. '*It is story time. You can lean against me in story time.*' '*When we sit in this chair, you can sit on my lap – but only when we sit in this chair.*'

Imitating intonation

Give opportunities for reciting or singing rhymes with actions.

- If the child begins to join in, recite or sing more slowly – if the child feels that they don't stand a chance of joining in, they will be more likely to give up.
- For older children, use nonsense rhymes and curriculum rhymes – as well as made up ditties.
- Exaggerate intonation as you recite/sing.

Verbalisation

- If the child copies words and repeats them, give opportunities for copying short phrases such as, '*I want bike*'.
- It may be helpful to have yes/no visual cards available, and practise using these with a nod or shake of the head. They are helpful when selecting from a choice of food, for example, at lunch or snack times.
- Mirrors are helpful for copying games with adults and peers and making face and mouth shape games.
- Increasingly, there are toys and games available that help children to co-ordinate their mouth and tongue muscles. Investigate these with the advice of a speech therapist.

Aspect 7: Non-verbal interaction

Letters	Body language	Communicating without speaking	Physical space	Intonation and word stress/expression
E	Responds to gesture to sit down	With prompting, indicates need with signs/symbols (e.g. Basic Makaton or PECS)	Can sit next to a peer leaving a small gap between them	Talks without monotone
E	Responds to gesture to stand up	Initiates communication using simple signs/symbols (e.g. Basic Makaton or PECS)	With reminders, knows not to sit on peers	Begins to recognise when own voice is too soft or too loud
F	Knows that eyes and body language communicate meaning	Observes speech activities	With reminders, knows not to climb on peers	Recognises an encouraging tone
F	Knows that clues are given with facial expressions	Attempts speech activities	Moves around the classroom avoiding climbing across peers	Responds to an encouraging tone
G	Recognises and responds to some signing by adults (e.g. Basic Makaton or PECS)	Uses single word communication accompanied by picture prompts	Can sit with a peer at a table	Uses encouraging tone with adults and peers
G	Recognises hand gesture for 'go away'	Uses single word communication with family or close peer	Understands concept of table space	Uses a cross tone appropriately but not excessively
H	Can tell if an adult's body stance is positive and approving	Interacts using a range of up to ten basic signs, with support, using PECS or Makaton	Sits on carpet/floor with a small group of peers	Uses rising intonation for questions
H	Can tell if an adult's body stance is negative and disapproving	Initiates interaction using a range of up to ten basic signs, using PECS or Makaton	Allows peers to have personal space on carpet	

Suggested activities or strategies

Makaton

Makaton is a simple signing language taught to children who are at the early stages of vocalisation. Unlike full sign languages, Makaton does not have its own grammar, because it is intended to be used to accompany oral language. Many young children with special needs are taught to use Makaton. For more information, visit: http://www.makaton.org/

PECS: Picture Exchange Communication System

PECS was created to encourage non-verbal AS children to communicate effectively using pictures. It is recommended that, in order to support children correctly, adults attend the two-day training course which teaches the progression of this technique. Once the child is using PECS successfully it is essential that the child's PECS book is with them at all times, as this is their 'voice'.

There are six phases involved in teaching a child to use PECS:

1 Adult withholds a desired item (such as a drink or toy) until the child requests it by giving the adult a single picture.
2 Child initiates communication by moving to the adult and offering the picture.
3 Child selects from a range of pictures and gives the chosen one to an adult.
4 Child selects two pictures: a symbol representing 'I want' and the desired object.
5 Child responds to the question 'What do you want?' by selecting the symbols/pictures for 'I want a ...'
6 Child's PECS vocabulary develops to comment on their environment (for example, 'pretty', 'cold').

As the child becomes more expert, they can begin to create increasingly complex sentences using PECS symbols.

For more information visit:
http://www.pecs.org.uk/general/what.htm

Supporting non-verbal communication

- Be overly expressive when using hand signals for 'Sit down', 'Come here' and so on. Makaton communication may be helpful, as some of the signs can be used in the classroom for all children and across the whole school community.
- Exaggerate body stances. If the child has made a wrong choice, use a cross voice. Accompany the words, 'No biting', with a cross face and gesture and a straight-backed, upright stance. It is sometimes helpful to state at this time, 'I'm cross, no biting'.
- Do not insist that the child speaks in school. Allow them to feel comfortable. Supply signs for 'toilet', 'yes', 'no' and so on, which can aid communication.
- If the child appears unwell it is helpful to have a visual of a body to point to if the child is unable to indicate on their body where the pain is.
- Encourage the child to use their method of communication; try not to pre-empt the situation.
- Give opportunities in play to practise changing their voice. Make a game with peers. For example, 'Can you ask Joseph for the car in a squeaky voice?'
- Use photographs of people making gestures – try to find matching pairs. Make a post box and post the correct pairs into the box. Talk about the gestures and what they mean and copy them.
- Set up a game with peers where no talking is allowed, only gestures. Play a game where one child directs another in gesture and the other follows: 'Come here', 'Sit down', 'Stand up', 'Go away'. Build up from one directed gesture to several.

Encouraging understanding of personal space

Use photographs to help the child to understand how to sit appropriately near peers. Indicate the right choice verbally and show them how to sit, correcting any errors. Use statements of reality. 'Look, Joseph is sitting next to Alice; he is not leaning on her.'

Letters	Body language	Communicating without speaking	Physical space	Intonation and word stress/expression
I	Makes some eye contact	Makes choices from adult-initiated rewards (e.g. selects from three options using PECS/Makaton)		Responds appropriately to some idioms (e.g. *'Hang on'*, *'Wait a minute'*)
I	Uses face to indicate lack of understanding	Offers choices to adult or peer from choice of two, using PECS/Makaton	Keeps appropriate distance from another's face when talking to familiar adult/peer	
J	Recognises encouraging body language in others to continue	Makes *'I see'* sentences using PECS/Makaton		Self-corrects own intonation
J	Recognises discouraging body language and ceases	Makes *'I hear'* sentences using PECS/Makaton	Keeps appropriate distance from another's face when talking to unfamiliar adult/peer	Knows that language includes idioms
K	Uses appropriate body language	Makes sentences using PECS/Makaton	Makes appropriate protest if own personal space is entered	Knows the meaning of ten common idioms
K	Recognises over-exaggerated body language	Makes sentences using PECS/Makaton and attempts to verbalise	Understands when not to enter personal space of others	Suggests where idioms could be used and when they may be funny
L	Recognises 'stop' signal	Communicates to a range of adults using PECS/Makaton	Knows how much personal space is needed in different contexts (e.g. dinner queue)	Asks questions to check the meaning of idioms
L	Can use 'stop' signal	Communicates to a range of peers using PECS/Makaton		

Suggested activities or strategies

Augmentative and Alternative Communication (AAC)

PECS and similar systems should be introduced after consultation with a communication specialist who may recommend PECS or suggest using a tablet computer together with an app such as Proloquo2Go, available to purchase from http://www.assistiveware.com/product/proloquo2go. With either system, the child will need to have it introduced gradually.

A lot of preparation by the adult is necessary to provide a suitable bank of vocabulary in PECS. In the first instance photographs are very helpful. A range of Communication in Print packages can be purchased to provide symbols such as http://www.widgit.com/; http://www.inclusive.co.uk/communicate-in-print-2-p2170; and www.visualaidsforlearning.com has some free downloadable symbols, as does www.twinkl.co.uk.

- It may be necessary to timetable specific planning and preparation time for PECS for the teaching assistant, as it is a time-consuming task.
- Once the child has mastered the art of *'I want'*, use everyday situations and books to teach *'I see'* and audio recordings and DVDs to teach *'I hear'*.
- Once the child is confident in using PECS with an adult, introduce a peer and then a small group of peers.
- It is a helpful exercise to introduce the whole class to PECS. During circle or carpet time set up the PECS strip for *'I want'* with two choices. This could easily be incorporated into fruit time when there is a choice of apple or pear. This will give the other children in the class an understanding of when it is their turn to respond.

Body language

Help the child to interpret body language.

- In social skills groups or circle time use DVDs to identify body language and talk about what it means and how the person feels.

- Use role-play to set up mime and freeze-frame activities imitating body language, using facial expressions and posture, and make this into a guessing game. For example, *'How is he feeling? How do you know?'*
- Use statements of reality to indicate body language. *'Look at the way Alice is walking, do you think she feels sad? How can we check? Look at her face.'*

Personal space

- If the pupil has a tendency to put their face too close to peers and make them feel uncomfortable, remind them that this is inappropriate and show them the appropriate distance.
- It may be necessary to give them a measure as a reference. *'If you cannot see the person's whole head you are too close.'*
- Use cartoon strip conversations and Social Stories™ to teach these social norms and allow opportunities to practise with an adult, a peer and a small group.

Talking and 'speed dating'

- Give opportunities for talking, modelling intonation and rhetoric, explaining how it is used and giving an opportunity to practise.
- Set up rotating conversation opportunities, like speed dating! Have a theme, which gives the child an opportunity to practise starting a conversation with an unfamiliar other, but in a safe, controlled environment. When the time is ended they move to the next person. Also, swap roles and allow the child to be the listener and make responses to keep the conversation going.
- Set up 'conversation bus stops'. Children are given starters for conversations such as, *'Where I went on holiday'*, or *'What I did at the weekend'*. Children continue the conversation and then report back what they have found out about the other person.
- Take opportunities to explore and explain idioms used in these informal contexts.

Letters	Body language	Communicating without speaking	Physical space	Intonation and word stress/expression
M	Uses signals of boredom	Meets needs by communication with a range of adults	Understands personal space on public transport	Understands simple sarcasm using low pitch (e.g. 'Nice weather' on a rainy day)
M	Recognises boredom in others	Meets needs by communication with a range of peers	Understands personal space in public toilets	Is able to use simple sarcasm using low pitch
N	Recognises aggressive/ intimidating body language	Communicates simply with familiar adults in unfamiliar social situations	Understands personal space in relation to opposite sex	Understands sarcasm using elongated words
N	Reacts appropriately to aggressive body language	Communicates simply with familiar peers in selected social situations	Responds appropriately to unexpected invasion of own personal space and that of others	Uses sarcasm by elongated words (e.g. 'Well excuuuuuse me')

Suggested activities or strategies

Responding to aggression

Teach children how to respond to aggressive behaviour in others.

- Using DVDs, offer opportunities to recognise intimidating/aggressive behaviour.
- Social Stories™ are helpful in teaching how to identify and react to aggression in others.
- Cartoon strip conversations are helpful in teaching how to react to aggressive language in others.
- In social skills groups, discussion and role-play can help teach appropriate reactions to aggressive behaviour and language in others.

Tricky social situations

Prepare the children for tricky situations such as using public toilets, or interacting with the opposite sex.

- In social skills groups, look at photographs of a variety of toilets. Discuss procedures and how this is different from home/school. Use school visits to practise, when an adult accompanies the class or group. For example, in the men's toilets it is not usual to stand and start a conversation, it is best to be efficient and come out quickly.
- As the child becomes older, acceptable distances change. The child may see girls and boys standing closer together or with linked arms or holding hands.
  - It is important to teach that this happens with the agreement of both parties. It is not acceptable to do this to a girl or boy just because you like them.
  - Teach ways of judging using facial expression, body language and talking.
- Social Stories™ are helpful to teach these rules, along with cartoon strip conversations.

- It is also important to teach that there are a range of alternative words to 'no', for example, '*Don't*', '*Get off*', '*I don't want to*', '*I don't like it*'.
- Explore situations in which one peer said '*Don't*' but the other continued. Discuss right/wrong choices and the feelings of those involved.
- Discuss wider issues in the community and the consequences of making the wrong choice.
- Model and teach skills such as how to get a conversation back on track, and how to change the topic politely. Opportunities for practising and a phrase bank are helpful.
- Prepare for changing social situations in school, such as party day, or Grandparents' lunch. Set up opportunities for social interaction with unfamiliar adults, for example, showing people to their seats, or waiting on tables.

Sarcasm and idioms

Explain to the child why and how sarcasm is used and how it is found amusing.

- An activity to unlock the hidden meaning of idioms is helpful. For example, '*If I said, "It is raining cats and dogs", would you run to the window to watch them falling from the sky?*'
- It may be helpful to draw an amusing version of the idiom, and then write its literal meaning.

There is a variety of commercial resources available to help children understand idioms.

Links to other *Target Ladders* titles

Other books in the Differentiating for Inclusion series may well include targets that will be appropriate for some AS children. For example:

Target Ladders: Behavioural, Emotional and Social Difficulties
Rachel Foulger, Sue Smallwood and Marion Aust

Includes additional targets for:
- Controlling emotions
- Managing transitions
- Taking responsibility
- Social interaction

Target Ladders: Dyslexia
Kate Ruttle

Includes additional targets for:
- Visual and auditory perception and memory
- Phonological awareness
- Reading comprehension and fluency
- Planning, organising and remembering

Target Ladders: Speech, Language and Communication Needs
Susan Lyon et al.

Includes additional targets for:
- Play and social interaction
- Attention control
- Comprehension
- Social communication

Other useful resources from LDA

How to Support and Teach Children on the Autism Spectrum
Dave Sherratt

Circle Time Kit
Jenny Mosley

Helping Children Deal with Anger
Jenny Mosley

Language Communication Pack
ASD Visual Aids

Socially Speaking (book and game)
Alison Schroeder

Pull Your Socks Up!